CAMBRIDGE LIBRARY COLLECTION

Books of enduring scholarly value

History

The books reissued in this series include accounts of historical events and movements by eye-witnesses and contemporaries, as well as landmark studies that assembled significant source materials or developed new historiographical methods. The series includes work in social, political and military history on a wide range of periods and regions, giving modern scholars ready access to influential publications of the past.

Journals Kept by Mr. Gully and Capt. Denham during a Captivity in China in the Year 1842

Published in 1844, this extraordinary book consists of the diaries of Robert Gully and Captain Denham, the Commander of the merchant vessel *Ann*, who were imprisoned in China in 1842, and notes exchanged between the two men (who were held captive in separate places). After some months of imprisonment, Gully was murdered, but Denham survived and was eventually released. The book, edited by 'a barrister' was designed to inform the British public of 'matters of which hitherto they have had slender but doubtful accounts', and to apply political and diplomatic pressure on the Chinese government, whose official account of the incident denied any wrong-doing by its representatives. Gully had distinguished himself in the taking of Ningpo during the Opium War of 1841–2, and later boarded the *Ann* to return to Macao. The vessel was subsequently wrecked off Formosa (Taiwan), where events related in the book occurred.

T0382518

Cambridge University Press has long been a pioneer in the reissuing of out-of-print titles from its own backlist, producing digital reprints of books that are still sought after by scholars and students but could not be reprinted economically using traditional technology. The Cambridge Library Collection extends this activity to a wider range of books which are still of importance to researchers and professionals, either for the source material they contain, or as landmarks in the history of their academic discipline.

Drawing from the world-renowned collections in the Cambridge University Library and other partner libraries, and guided by the advice of experts in each subject area, Cambridge University Press is using state-of-the-art scanning machines in its own Printing House to capture the content of each book selected for inclusion. The files are processed to give a consistently clear, crisp image, and the books finished to the high quality standard for which the Press is recognised around the world. The latest print-on-demand technology ensures that the books will remain available indefinitely, and that orders for single or multiple copies can quickly be supplied.

The Cambridge Library Collection brings back to life books of enduring scholarly value (including out-of-copyright works originally issued by other publishers) across a wide range of disciplines in the humanities and social sciences and in science and technology.

Journals Kept by Mr. Gully and Capt. Denham during a Captivity in China in the Year 1842

Robert Gully
Captain Denham

Cambridge
University Press

CAMBRIDGE UNIVERSITY PRESS

Cambridge, New York, Melbourne, Madrid, Cape Town,
Singapore, São Paolo, Delhi, Mexico City

Published in the United States of America by Cambridge University Press, New York

www.cambridge.org
Information on this title: www.cambridge.org/9781108045711

This edition first published 1844
This digitally printed version 2012

ISBN 978-1-108-04571-1 Paperback

JOURNALS

KEPT BY

MR. GULLY AND CAPT. DENHAM

DURING A

CAPTIVITY IN CHINA

IN THE YEAR 1842.

EDITED BY A BARRISTER.

LONDON:

CHAPMAN AND HALL, 186, STRAND.

YORK: J. L. LINNEY.

1844.

NOTE.

December 5, 1843.—The Indian Mail, which has just arrived, has brought the Report of the Chinese authorities on the Inquiry they were ordered to make respecting the murder of the crews of the Nerbudda and Ann. This Inquiry was undertaken on the demand of Sir H. Pottinger. The Report is ridiculously defective in every respect but one; namely, in that which declares the authorities at Formosa to have obtained from the Emperor rewards and honours, by fraudulently and falsely representing the mode of the capture of the two unfortunate crews. The parties thus guilty are doomed to punishment. On this point it is plain enough, and so far it fully confirms the statements made in the Journals of Mr. Gully and Captain Denham. Those Journals will furnish, if the Chinese think fit to use them, the means of obtaining fuller information on other points. And it is even yet to be hoped, that they who caused the murder of so many of the captives, will be at least equally punished with those who won honours and rewards by false representations. The Chinese government should be pressed to make further inquiries.

INTRODUCTION.

THE following pages are chiefly composed of the Diary of Mr. Robert Gully, a fine, gallant, and excellent-hearted young man, who, after enduring an imprisonment of some months in a Chinese jail, was barbarously murdered. He had been engaged in commercial pursuits but quitted them for a time to join the British expedition. He was on board the Nemesis, and honourably distinguished himself at the taking of Ningpo, and in the other actions in which that vessel was engaged. His amiable manners, as well as his undaunted courage, won him the esteem and friendship of the officers of the expedition, whose dangers and whose glories he shared, and by all of whom the necessity for his return to the occupations which first brought him to China was sincerely regretted. In order to return to Macao he put himself on board the Anne, a merchant vessel, which was afterwards wrecked on the island of Formosa, where the events related in this Diary occurred, and where his life was at length cruelly taken by his barbarous captors. A gallant fellow-captive, (Capt.

Denham, commander of the Ann) who happily escaped the same cruel end, but who underwent similar sufferings, and was in one instance very savagely treated, also kept a Diary, and his labours will be employed to render the narrative unbroken, and to continue it after the death of his companion. These Diaries are offered to the public with the view of informing them as to matters of which hitherto they have had but slender and doubtful accounts.

Notwithstanding a commercial intercourse of many years' duration, our knowledge of the Chinese was but small. Their absurd jealousy of foreigners and contempt for them; the fact, that what we wanted in the way of trade could be procured without any direct diplomatic intercourse, and the few cases of necessity that arose for more intimate acquaintance with them, left us much in the dark as to their habits and manners. Of their laws and of the mode of administering them, there was happily for a long time but little cause for seeking knowledge. But at length two or three cases occurred which allowed no room to doubt, that whatever chance of justice or protection the law afforded to the subjects of China, foreigners were not to expect it to yield them any such advantage. Indeed Mr. Davies, in his excellent work on the Chinese, distinctly states their explicit avowal, that whenever foreigners came under the criminal jurisdiction of the Chinese authorities, they must submit with implicit obedience, not to what the laws had provided, but to what the Chinese officers thought fit to order. The cases of foreigners were those not for the operation of the laws, but cases of exception to their operation; in the instance of an offending foreigner, the laws were declared to be suspended, and the will of the authorities assumed their place. It is somewhat strange that so many and such gallant nations whose citizens visited China, and who would quarrel among themselves on the slightest provocation, should have submitted for so many years to a jurisdiction so capricious in itself, and, as experience proved it, so cruel in its operation. The great demand for the staple article of the Chinese trade, the large profits made by those who engaged in it, the great distance of China from Europe (a circumstance more important formerly than at present), and a vague notion perhaps that the conquest of a people so indefinitely numerous would be impossible, and the coercion of them by any thing short of actual conquest absolutely hopeless, no doubt contributed to produce this result. The people of each country treated with indifference the loss of an individual subject or an individual insult offered by the Chinese to their flag. The locality of the wrong was distant—the bitterness of it had died away before the knowledge of it had reached to Europe—the means of redress were difficult, and the inconvenience that would be suffered from a stoppage of the trade considerable. No nation, therefore, put itself in the position of one seeking justice and demanding right from the Chinese. The matters of complaint that did arise were neglected—the recurrence of them was sought to be avoided or evaded, and the Chinese were left in possession of what seemed to them to be an absolute, unquestioned, and unlimited authority over the persons of those who traded to their shores. The consuls of the different nations resided on those shores, less as the honoured and powerful representatives of their respective countries, than as authorized solicitors for justice or mercy from the Chinese officials.

This was a monstrous evil in itself, and its consequences were fearful. There can be no doubt that it occasioned much suffering that never became known to the European public; that it engendered on the part of the Chinese a state of insolent self-sufficiency that was continually felt even in quiet times, but that became doubly outrageous when a condition of tolerated commerce was converted by circumstances into one of national hostility. These pages will exhibit a sad instance of this truth.

It was impossible that this state of things could continue for ever. The increasing trade with China increased the probabilities of some event occurring which would compel one or other of the European nations to stand upon its rights;—the rights of civilization—and to demand and enforce a recognition of them from the Chinese government. In the affairs of this world, it often happens that the attainment of the most desirable objects is promoted by the least desirable means. It was so in the case of our relations with China. The purchase of opium by the Chinese, was only effected by a kind of recognised smuggling, which filled the pockets of the Chinese officials, but brought nothing into the public treasury, and could not be made the subject of lawful barter. The Sycee silver, therefore, as one of their officials expressed it, "oozed out" of the country in a way quite puzzling to the Chinese emperor and his ministers, and what appeared to be the most direct, and the only way of stopping its outflowing, was at once adopted. The opium trade was forbidden under the severest penalties. But these were attempted to be enforced almost alone against foreigners. And in accordance with the universal practice of what is called "a paternal government," extreme violence of threatened punishment was deemed the sole means of rendering law efficient for its intended purpose. If the Chinese government had had power enough, the severest measures, including torture itself, would have been tried upon the English residents at Canton; but they existed there in numbers, were under the eye of a government officer, who had the power to afford them protection; and the indiscriminate persecution and murder of men, women, and children, thus circumstanced, was therefore impossible. What the government could do it did; and the ferocity which could not be safely gratified at Canton, was vented on persons entirely innocent of engaging in the opium trade, but whom chance threw into the hands of the Chinese. The triumphs that could not be obtained over the English forces in fair fight, were sought and found, and abused in the case of shipwrecked mariners. The Nerbudda, a merchant vessel, had been wrecked on the coast of the Island of Formosa. The vessel was plundered, the crew seized and imprisoned—what were the privations and the tortures which the men of that vessel underwent, the public have not yet been informed. The Narratives of Mr. Gully and Captain Denham will show what were those inflicted on other shipwrecked men. The Ann, on its voyage from Chusan to Macao, was lost on the night of the 10th of March, 1842, upon the same Island of Formosa. The manner of the capture was such as would have disgraced wreckers pursuing their unholy as well as unlawful and punishable trade; yet it was effected, not by a mere set of lawless vagabonds, but by the Chinese civil and military authorities. The vessel was plundered and broken up, and the unhappy men stripped perfectly naked, were forced upon a long and toilsome and painful march. Some of them died under the infliction. For the details of these cruelties we refer to the narratives themselves, only observing with pleasure, and it is the solitary instance of pleasure that the circumstances afford the reader, that the female sex even in that barbarous country, and in spite of every thing that might have led any one to anticipate a different behaviour, asserted its wonted sympathy with the unfortunate. After a march of many days the unhappy captives arrived at the prison in which they were to be detained. Here they were divided, and the two narratives are extremely interesting, from the insight they give us into the habits and manners of the Chinese towards prisoners.

The government of China is one of those called paternal governments; that is to say, it claims and exercises the absolute and irresistible control supposed to be vested in a father over his children, without having one particle of his good feelings to restrain its abuse. Such a government is always the worst that can be imagined. It assumes its authority to be an emanation from the Deity, and is proportionably severe and cruel towards any that even appear to contradict the assumption. Its supreme will is the only law it recognises, and in administering that law it makes no account of the feelings, wishes, or necessities of men submitted to its control. The two narratives which are in the form of logbooks or diaries will exhibit, as might be expected, the most capricious changes from severity to kindness, and from kindness to severity, according as one or another man, or as the same man in a particular temper had to deal with the prisoners. From day to day the poor captives were in expectation of hearing from Macao or Amoy. They bribed persons to deliver letters, and there is no doubt that one of these letters was delivered. It was acknowledged and answered. Yet assistance never came. Those who were suffering the pains of a severe imprisonment and the tortures of hope deferred, blamed the English authorities for weakness if not indifference. It would be matter of the deepest regret to be obliged to believe that either Sir Henry Pottinger or any, even an undistinguished Englishman, could have been indifferent to the fate of his fellow-creatures and fellow-countrymen. And the daily and hourly falsehoods of the Chinese, suggest a state of circumstances that seems to excuse the English authorities. It is plain that upon the receipt of the letter that was acknowledged there was a mighty stir among the Chinese. Mandarins of high rank came to examine the prisoners. Rumours were spread of their being about to be removed up the country, and the care and suspicion of the jailers were doubled. The probability is that the English authorities, on the receipt of this letter, had had communications with the Chinese, and had demanded the prisoners, offering ransom or exchange, or perhaps threatening to come and take them. The course the Chinese would adopt under such circumstances is plain. They would solemnly declare that the prisoners had been removed, and were well treated. And without further information being conveyed to the British authorities, they would be deceived by these representations, and might even have been misled by false information into seeking the unhappy captives at a place where they could not be found. This is what all would hope to be the fact, for it would indeed be painful to believe that the glory which Sir H. Pottinger has acquired in China bore upon its surface the dark spot of an inhuman indifference to the lives of any of his countrymen in the narratives themselves, full as they are of proofs of distress.

The conduct of the Chinese towards the crew of the Ann ended as it had begun. The English were represented as captives to the valour of the Chinese sailors and troops; honours were by this falsehood obtained from the Emperor, and then, whether by his orders, or because it so pleased the capricious barbarity of the mandarins of the place, all those who were not official persons in the ship, which of course included Mr. Gully, were privately murdered. His diary stops abruptly, but a scrap of paper, written as it is believed, on the day of his murder, and probably forming the very last sentence that he ever wrote, indicates the spirit and courage, the gaiety even, with which, up to the last, he bore his misfortunes. This little scrap of paper shows too that at the moment he wrote it, he had no anticipation of the intended murder; and in all probability he was hurried from one of the ordinary occupations of his prison to the place of execution. The death of this excellent young man must yet form the subject of serious representation to the Chinese government, and if falsehood should not succeed in baffling every demand for justice, retribution must yet overtake his murderers.

JOURNAL

KEPT BY MR. GULLY.

March 8th, 1842.—We left Chusan on the morning of the 8th of March 1842, in the brig Ann, for Macao, intending to return again in time to see Pekin taken. We anchored at night off Keeto Point, there being no wind.

9th.—Under weigh at daylight, and fell in with the Lynx and Arun about 8 a.m., and after receiving some treasure from the former, made sail for Symoon. During the day the breeze freshened, and in the evening, being off the entrance to Symoon, Captain Denham determined not to run the risk of losing a fair breeze, and altered the brig's course, so as to be well clear of the land before dark, shortly after passing it; starboard tack. In the morning we passed an English vessel working to windward; think it was the Hooghley.

10th.—Breeze increasing, with thick cloudy weather; so much so that we did not get an observation. Capt. Denham worked the dead reckoning every three or four hours; and on my going to bed he calculated we were about 30 or 40 miles from the mainland: and I perfectly recollect (although I don't think I said so at the time) that I considered Capt. Denham was steering a course likely to take him rather too near to Ockseu* and the islands about there; but it did not prevent my sleeping, for I knew the waters were bold on that shore, and that there was an extra look-out kept. A little after 12 a.m. (as I afterwards learned), I was roused up by feeling the vessel strike the ground. I jumped up immediately and rushed on deck, when she struck again much heavier than before, and a tremendous sea came over her starboard quarter and went clean forward, carrying away the small boat at the starboard, davits and all the loose spars. The men were then aloft on the main topsail yard. Capt. Denham, who was the first person I saw on reaching the deck, was endeavouring to get the lascars to work, but at last was obliged to call the sea-cunnies off the topsail yard. Sea followed sea clean over, and I gave it up for lost. She appeared to be breaking up fast, and making sure we were off the Ockseu Island, I looked over the side, and said to myself, "It is

* Mr. Gully afterwards states his opinion that the land is laid down wrongly in the charts, and that the channel is narrower than has been supposed.—See Post, March 17.

hard to die at my age." I then saw land on the larboard side quite plain, close to. All this time she had been forging ahead fast, and the sea continued to strike her so heavily, that it was with the greatest difficulty any person could hold on. I went aft, and saw that her whole stern frame was gone. The masts were then cut away, and we then lay quite easy, but knew there was no hope of saving the brig, for the water was up to the cabin deck, and the water-casks floating about the main hold; we determined (thinking we were inside one of the Ockseu Islands) at daylight to land, and search for a boat, so that some of us might get to Chin Chew for assistance. To effect this the powder magazines were got up, but we found the powder all damaged by water, as well as the cartridges for the brig's guns. Employed until daylight making cartridges out of some fine powder belonging to Captain Denham, and a little taken from one or two large cartridges which, with a few the gunner had in his berth, made up about four cartridges to each musket. I then turned in for a short nap, after shifting my wet clothes, and sending out others to whoever was in want, my chest being dry. At daylight our mistake about being inside the Ockseus was very plain, for we saw the low shore stretching to the southward as far as we could see, and high hills about fifteen miles in shore. This told us plain enough that we were on Formosa which was shortly after confirmed by a man whom we brought on board, but from his language we could make nothing of him. As soon as it got well light we saw the little jolly-boat about a quarter of a mile in shore of us, bottom up. The brig was lying on her starboard broadside on a shingly beach, mingled with rocks here and there. About a quarter of a mile outside of her was a line of breakers running parallel with the shore as far as we could see. This we must have been driven over; luckily we had not struck there or great numbers of us must have perished. We did not see a single opening large enough for the long-boat to pass. This boat was prepared over night with provisions, compass, sails, &c. The remaining cutter was stove in by the hands who cleared the long-boat, and afterwards received the *coup de grace* from the fall of the foremast. Under these circumstances our only chance of saving either lives or property appeared to be to seize some junk or junks, and for that purpose we determined to set out, all of us, for to have left any one on board must have been folly. The brig was then high and dry, and the tide making. From the over-night's experience we doubted if she would stand another tide, and there were only fifty-seven of us, and we had already proved the lascars to be of no use at all in an emergency. Our surmise about the danger of stopping during high-water proved afterwards to be true, for we have since heard that twenty-five Chinese were drowned by trying it. We then started about 7 a. m., taking with us nothing but our arms, nautical instruments, a "Norie," and a few extra clothes on our backs, and a spy-glass. All being together, Capt. Denham gave particular instructions for all hands to keep together, and not be straggling. We commenced our march over a level sandy uncultivated plain thickly intersected with clear freshwater streams, and here and there a house, but no signs of any town. We soon descried the masts of some junks, at a good distance off to the northward, and made for them in double-quick time; and on reaching them found them moored in a small creek, at low water not the breadth across of the length of one of them. They were about two miles from the wreck, as near as I could judge. The crew of the largest were at chow chow, and readily offered us what they had, and no resistance was made to our coming on board. Part of us went into the large one, and a part into the second: there were four or five altogether. We needed no boat to get on board, for the creek was not deeper than our knees. The junks were all deeply laden with rice. It was then blowing a strong gale right into the entrance of the creek, and we saw that our only chance (the wind not shifting or abating) would not turn up that day. We commenced with the help of the shroffs to hire the junk man to take us over to Chin Chew. He said he was not going to start for ten days, but would go and speak to the head man. We offered him 3000 dollars for a passage over. To add to our miseries it now began raining, and we had very little covering except the mat roof to the junk, and there were more than could stow under it. What our feelings were cannot be described. On an enemy's coast, without ammunition to defend ourselves for a few hours, even if we were sure of the wind abating—and we saw no prospect of it. On the walk to the junk one of our party straggled and was taken by the Chinese, but not badly treated. Shortly after our getting on board the junk, small parties of armed men were continually collecting on the north shore of the creek, and about eleven o'clock two respectable-looking men came down to the water's edge, and beckoned us to come on shore, but we declined. They then went to the shore as close to the sea as they could, and appeared to be looking at the wreck. The rain coming on they went away. They were attended by a number of soldiers, and a large posse of men armed with different weapons, who I think were also soldiers with their jackets turned inside out, to hide their uniforms during acts of plunder. Here were about 3000 or 4000 altogether. For a long time they contented themselves with using threatening gestures. They then gave us a good stoning, which amazed the junk people. They threatened to take the anchors up which were buried in the shingle ashore. One fellow in particular was very active in his manœuvres; one of the junkmen requested us to shoot him, but we declined, for we saw no chance of getting the junks out of the creek, and to have commenced hostilities with only four rounds of cartridge each would have been folly; for, from the nature of the ground, they could have stoned us out of the junk from behind the adjoining sand-bank without our being able to return an effective shot. We were thus compelled to wait and trust to chance. We did not give ourselves up, because from their gestures we made sure of instant death. When the rain commenced, the whole body of men went behind the beach for shelter until the afternoon, when the tide beginning to fall they were joined by more soldiers and a mandarin in a chair, who likewise took shelter under the bank. At low water they sallied forth and boarded all the junks; and from their not showing any hesitation, I think they must have known, from inspection of the wreck, that the powder was all damaged. We had nothing else for it but to put up with our lot. We were stripped of nearly every rag, some of us to the skin. They left me nothing but two pairs of old drawers. I never felt the cold so severe in my life, and endeavoured to get down the small hatch into the cabin; but on putting my legs down, they were immediately so belaboured that I was glad to haul them up. The Chinese shroffs, &c., were not stripped. When the wretches had done their work effectually, one of them waved a handkerchief which was answered from the beach. The mandarin in the chair came over, made a show of dispersing the mob, and we were then all taken out of the junk except one China-boy who was never heard of afterwards. Each was put under the charge of two or three soldiers, and we commenced the most miserable and painful marches with no covering, and a piercing northerly wind with rain and sleet, no shoes, and most of the way over the beach composed entirely of shingle, covered with old cockle and mussel shells, which cut the feet at every step, and often I was compelled to go on my hands and knees to ease the pain of my feet. Our march was in a southerly direction: we passed the brig, and beheld a most annoying scene of plunder; for a great distance round the spot parties in soldiers' clothes were coming and going with sheets of copper, some with boxes of dollars, chests of drawers, boxes, clothes, &c. Some of our people slipped away from their guards, and went away on board, hoping to find some articles of clothing, but they were all disappointed. The decks were broken up; every thing moveable gone; and parties employed getting the kentledge out of the after-hold. We crossed several small streams on our way, and about six o'clock, or just before dusk, we crossed a rather larger one, with junks moored as in the first one, the water about up to our middle. There was a small town on the south side of it; and here we were halted and put into a small barn, in which was a quantity of paddy husk; and glad we were, after suffering so much, to bury ourselves in it, after drinking some cunjle which was brought; but we could get no dry clothes. The distance marched over such dreadful ground, was, I think, about six miles. Several of our party were missing; and it did not surprise us on the following morning to learn that Samuel, the Lascar cook and second-mate's servant, had perished on the road from pain and fatigue. A third, William, sea-cunny, was brought in a basket senseless from cold and fatigue. The others missing were some sea-cunnies and the gunner, whom we afterwards learned were taken to an inferior mandarin's house, and much better treated.

11th and 12th.—Still blowing a gale of wind with rain. This day we were crowded with visiters. Rice and congou given us three times a day, and on making a survey we found there were a few of the lascars who, by getting under the stern of the junks, had preserved the clothes with which they had left the brig, and as they nearly all had a double suit, we (Captain Denham, Mr. Roope, and myself) got a portion of them. I got a pair of trousers and shirt; but all were not so fortunate, for the serang and some others refused to give a rag although they had three suits.

13th.—Still blowing hard but not so much rain. Heard continual rows all day long outside in the streets, and observed the shops all closed. Our guards told us it was about us, but left us to imagine why. In the evening we were shifted to a sort of joss-house, with granaries at the back. Our sleeping-place was one of the granaries, but so small for our number that we got very little sleep. Our food here, for the time, consisted of salt fish, greens, and rice; three things that if I could get dry bread and water I never would touch, and which I believe have been the cause of my sickness.

14th.—Shortly after breakfast we heard a noise outside, and saw spears and flags. Our guards told us we were going away. One of them called Mr. Roope aside, and took him up a ladder where he sung out to me for assistance. Captain Denham and myself went up to him and found the soldier trying to persuade Mr. Roope to go up stairs, and made motions for us not to go out to the mandarins. We went up to a small clean room, where the man wanted us to remain, but thinking it was only for the purpose of plunder that he wished to keep us, we determined to go with the rest. Perhaps the fellow had heard of our offer to the junkman and really meant well, but it was difficult to judge. We were then all taken before three mandarins, tickets put round our necks, and we were marched under a strong escort of soldiers to a small walled town inland about three miles. The walls were of round stones and chunam. We passed from one end of the town to the other, where we were seated under the walls close to a mandarin's office for about half an hour, I suppose for the people to have a good look at us. We were then taken into the mandarin's premises and divided into two parties, the soldiers having previously told us we were going to be beheaded, which I should have believed if they had not overdone the thing by beginning to sharpen their swords on the stones. We were put into two cells about eight feet by seven each, in each of which were stowed twenty-five of us and three jailers or guards. The weather extremely cold, nothing to lay our heads on, and nothing but a sprinkling of straw to keep us from the damp bricks. The land on each side of the road was cultivated and rice growing, the fields were very small, and only divided by a low round embankment about one foot high. The villages appeared to be pretty, from their being surrounded by bamboo. Here, for the first time, I saw a wheeled cart, but we had before noticed the marks of wheels on our first march. It was a very clumsy affair, drawn by a bullock. It was passing across the ploughed ground for no reason that I could see except that there was no other road. The wheels were composed of two solid pieces of wood joined together in the centre, with a hole which merely slipped on to the axle-tree and was confined by a linch-pin. The cart was of bamboo. The wheels made very curious gyrations in their passage through the mud. In the villages we were stared at by every body, women and all. The women were unaccountably plain even for Chinese women, both here and through all parts of the island I have seen, but they have a very pretty fashion of wearing natural flowers in their hair. On our road we passed several parties employed carrying the brig's guns in the same direction that we were travelling. Altogether, I think under other circumstances I should have enjoyed this trip much, but my feet were so painful with the sores of our former march that I could not. As it was, it was a great relief after the crowded granary, and I think did me good.

15th. Nothing of any moment occurred except that we were joined by the gunner and sea-cunnies, missing up to this time. They had been much better treated than ourselves, and had clothes given to them, though rather of a fantastic nature. The treatment may, perhaps, be partly attributed to their thinking the gunner to be some great man, from his having a mermaid marked on his arm, in the way common among sea-faring people. They partly laboured under this mistake up to this present meeting. Both this day and the 16th we were crowded by visiters, who were a great nuisance. The government people who came, all told the same lie,—viz., that we were going to be sent away in a junk. One fellow took the trouble to draw me on one side to explain it more clearly. If we ever placed reliance in their words we were undeceived on the evening of the 17th, for we were then all taken before the mandarins, ticketed, a fresh name given to each, and ornamented with handcuffs, we were placed in chairs and conveyed out of the town. We passed outside, and for some miles over a country tolerably cultivated. We were told in the villages we passed through that we were going to have our heads taken off. During the passage my bearers capsized my chair three times, which was occasioned by the slippery state of the footpath. I enjoyed this much more than the bearers, who got a good blowing up from the soldiers by whom we were attended every time it happened. At last they persuaded the man who had charge of the key of my handcuffs to allow me to walk, which I agreed to do as long as the road continued soft. (The man with the key attended me all the way to Tywan-foo.) I was glad enough to take advantage of the permission to walk. I particularly observed that the soldiers in many instances carried a very superior kind of matchlock to any I had seen in China before, and they were kept in much better order. The barrels were cut outside, six square, and as well as the bore were quite smooth and bright. Some again were wretched-looking beings with rusty spears, shields and old caps without any stiffening in the borders. These I conjectured were the militia, the others regulars. A short time after I observed wheat growing, but the crops were only small and poor in comparison to those common in England. This was the case throughout the whole journey to this town, and I dare say the Chinese understand as little about growing wheat or barley as our farmers know about rice. We soon came to a very barren description of country, interesting to geologists only. Immense plains stretching inland as far as we could see, composed of round stones, the same as we call "boulders" in Yorkshire, with hills or mountains formed of the same, no vegetation being visible except now and then a green spot on the very tops of the hills, the first of which was some miles from the sea. Up to the time of our wreck I had always imagined the shore of Formosa to be very bold from having seen these hills often while at sea. The land, between them and the sea, is so very low and without trees that it must be very deceiving to any one at sea, and I doubt very much if the channel as laid down in the charts is not too wide. During this, our first trip in sedans, we were shown many little roadside public houses, where we were taught how to spend our mace by the man who had charge of each. These houses, together with every building we passed, were formed of the before-mentioned boulders and mud, with, in many instances, a large wide-spreading tree or trees with seats close to them. The country had a most wild and heavy aspect, more so than any I ever saw, and I began to think Formosa a sad misnomer. The scattered houses were few and far between, and the people appeared a more wretched ill-clothed race than I ever saw in China before. This day's march, altogether in a southerly direction, was about twenty-five miles; we crossed several streams running to the westward, all of which were evidently smaller than at some other seasons of the year. We also passed several small towns not walled, or if so, the walls were only of mud, but all had gates, one a brick one, the others bamboo. We suffered all sorts of abuse and indignities in passing through these, as well as all the others throughout the whole journey; *but the women did not join in this*, although they showed the usual curiosity of the sex. We arrived at our halting-place, a large town with high walls made of brick, about dusk; for some miles previous to getting there, the country was a continued paddy swamp interspersed with small hamlets, surrounded with bamboo, which grows here larger than I ever saw in other places. I have noticed it full sixty feet high. I found, on minute inspection, that the axletrees of the wheeled carts turned with the wheels. The bazaar of this town appeared well furnished with fish. We observed the mast heads of several junks a short distance to the westward, and these were the only signs of the sea that met our eye until we got close to Tywanfoo.

17th.—The crowd of gazers was very annoying, and it was even a relief when we found ourselves lodged in the common jail, formed of wooden bars, like some of our English cages in country towns, and with the same furniture inside; viz., stocks, &c. We were stowed in two of these places, with a third empty between us, and a view of some Chinese prisoners in front, in the same sort of place. It rained nearly the whole time we were here, and the cold was very severe; our food abominable. Captain Denham was taken before the mandarins and examined as to the nature of his ship, his business and other questions, and on his insisting that he had only sixty hands in all, they threatened to beat him. The shroff and carpenter were both thrashed most unmercifully, and consoled us by giving it as their opinion, that we should all lose our heads. They said the mandarins were determined to make the brig out to be a man of war, coming to look after the crew of the Nerbudda, the crew of which we were told from the first were still on the island, but we did not believe it; it turned out afterwards however to be true. Captain Denham tried at first to make the brig out as one belonging to America, but the mandarins burst out laughing at him, and soon proved that they knew exactly what she was, but that it was not what they wished to make her out. Opium smoking is carried on quite publicly here, and some of the soldiers who composed our escort, wore their opium pipes in their girdles.

19th.—I was roused up about the middle of the night by the carpenter, shroff, and a strange Chinaman. The first requested me to get up and write a letter to Captain Smith at Amoy, that a junk was going over, and if I could tell Captain Smith to give the bearer 50 dollars on receipt of it, it would go safe. Immediately I commenced with a China pencil and paper which they had for the purpose, and soon finished it. I told Captain Smith that we were going to the capital of the island, Tywanfoo; this I had learnt from the carpenter. A few minutes after they had left the jail the carpenter returned and asked if we could give the man a few dollars now to assist him in getting a passage. We told him we had none, which was the truth. This question immediately damped all our hopes, for we guessed the whole thing to be a trap to get money. I forgot to mention that the interpreter between Captain Denham and the mandarins was a Chinaman, by name Ayum, who had been some time at Singapore and picked up a little smattering of Hindostanee and English. He turned out to be a great scoundrel afterwards, and gave his own answers where his knowledge of the language would not permit him to ask the questions put by the mandarins, or where he did not like the answers. He made himself very noisy and officious during the whole journey. I omitted to mention that at the first walled town we were in I obtained paper and ink, and commenced a log, but it only existed two days, for Mr. Roope, who had charge of it, was taken into a separate room, strictly searched, and it was taken from the lining of a China jacket he had on while under examination. Captain Denham was allowed to wash his face, and a towel and some dinner given to him, but we did not enjoy the luxury of a wash from the time we left the brig until two days after leaving this town, and then only on the road where we stopped a few minutes to eat; the mandarins who accompanied us continually hurrying the bearers. I may here mention that the remaining four marches averaged from 20 to 25 miles per day, as near as I could guess.

21st.—We resumed our journey as before, but leg irons were added to our handcuffs, which put an end to our walking. The country from this town to the capital improved in appearance every march, although some parts of it were wild and dreary enough. We crossed several large streams; the one we crossed this day by means of a ferry boat. All the others of any size were very shallow but strong, and were crossed by means of bamboo rafts, the chairs being placed on them with their contents, and if any thing had happened to the ferry boat or the rafts, we must have been drowned, with our handcuffs and leg irons on. Besides these, we crossed by means of rickety bridges, the dry courses of many torrents, which from all appearance, at some other time of the year must have come down in great strength, and in two or three instances we crossed on foot dry shod, courses two or three hundred yards broad, which the water had made for itself, through paddy fields, &c., sweeping all before it. Before leaving the last town we had two mace given us each, to buy our food on the road, and we were told it was to last two days. I may here mention, that although cheated by the man who had charge of me, I lived much better on one mace a day than in their prisons. We arrived before sunset at another walled town, and were taken to a large joss-house, which was prepared with straw for us, and here I had the most comfortable night's rest of any since the brig was lost, my handcuffs being taken off during the night. I had previously broken one pair at the last town, because they would not take them off at night.

22d.—We started again early in the morning, passing through a country very highly cultivated, with here and there a patch of common, with bullocks feeding, and there were graves in great numbers precisely like our own; but very few did I see throughout the whole journey, with the usual Chinese-shaped tombstones. The weather now was very hot, and in consequence of the complaints of my bearers concerning my weight, I was allowed three, being one more than the rest. The face of the country reminded me a good deal of some parts of Cambridgeshire, near Newmarket, where hedges are scarce, and the fields are bounded by belts of firs or a ditch. From the use of wheeled carts, of course the roads were wider than usual in China, and made the similitude to Cambridgeshire greater. Some of the lanes were shaded for miles by high bamboos on each side. A great deal of ground was covered with the sugar-cane, and we passed several mills or places for preparing the sugar during the journey. Tobacco also is grown in large quantities, and a sort of vine, very carefully grown on trellis-work of bamboo, in rows, generally fenced in, and a mat covering for each row. I could not learn the name of it; I thought at the time it was pepper, but believe I was mistaken. It was generally grown close to the houses of the cultivators, and more care seemed to be taken of it than any thing else. What it was I cannot imagine. The women on all occasions ran out to look at the foreigners, and I never saw so plain a set. I did not see a decent face until I reached the capital, but they looked clean in most instances. In the evening we arrived at a large town with chunammed walls, and at the place we entered there was a sort of outer gate, some hundred yards from the one to the town, where there were two very long iron guns placed on the ground, I suppose for us to see. We were taken to a jail-yard, and a mandarin with a brass button came to see us eat some rice and fish provided for us, but as far as Capt. Denham, Mr. Roope, and myself were concerned, he was disappointed, for it was so filthily dirty that we refused it. They then showed us our place of rest for the night, another cage. We remonstrated that there was nothing but the bars between us and the China prisoners, that it was not large enough, &c., but to no purpose; and the mandarin flew into an awful passion, strutted about pulling his mustaches, and looking exactly as laughable as I have seen would-be tyrants in Richardson's booth at Newcastle fair. I gave him a look that brought his attendants about me. Into the place we went, and I had to try and sleep with my head close to the buckets of the Chinese prisoners. As they refused to take my handcuffs off, I again broke them. Here the serang, who had during the cold weather refused all applications, offered the gunner one of his four shirts, a blanket one, but it was so filled with vermin, that the gunner threw it away. This serang and several others behaved very disgracefully throughout. Very different was the conduct of my boy Francis, who, during the whole of our luckless imprisonment, up to this time, has behaved as well as any one could behave. Until the middle of the night, when I spoke through the bars to our Chinese, I thought this was Tywanfoo, and glad enough I was to find I was mistaken. I slept very little.

23d.—This morning we were all taken out and two mace given to each, and a new pair of handcuffs to me; but nothing was said about breaking the others, or if there was I did not understand them. The country this day was under the same kind of cultivation as heretofore, but more thickly studded with trees, and the ground was rather higher than usual. I think we steered more inland this day. At our bamboo ferry, while waiting for my turn, which, although with three bearers, was always last, I had an opportunity of saying a few words to the young shroff, whose chair was placed next to mine. He was in irons as well as myself, with the addition of a chain round his neck, and in such a fright, that I could get nothing from him except that we were going to get our heads taken off. This night we stopped in a large village, at a public eating-house, or rather a post-house, for there were numbers of chairs like our own, I suppose for hire. They seemed to be carrying on a good business, and had great difficulty in accommodating us, and regular fights took place among the Chinese for food, of which there was a scarcity for some time. One fellow got a bloody nose, and rushed to the mandarin who accompanied us, with his face covered with blood, crying like a great baby; this made us all laugh, I think for the first time together, since the 10th. This mandarin was far more civil than the one at the last town, and turned some families out of a decent room with tressel beds, and allowed us to occupy it. We also had our irons taken off, at least I had. The others (Captain Denham and Mr. Roope) could take theirs off at pleasure. I never was lucky enough to get a lock of that kind. I have learned from Captain Denham that a mandarin with a white button (we had met several on this day's march) had stopped to speak to him, gave him something to eat, and told him not to fear, that they were not going to cut our heads off. This, of course, was by signs. I slept very well this night. The soldiers slept in the open shop as usual, amusing themselves with their opium pipes. The country-people we passed on the road had most curious pipes made of bamboo, the root forming the bowl, which in all cases was so small that it would hardly hold a good pinch of snuff. The roots were crooked, like a hocky-stick, with the bowl on the inside. The pipe altogether was often five feet long, as thick as a man's wrist, and used as a walking-stick.

24th.—At daylight we started over a more hilly country than before, and many of the sides of the hills not far inland were well wooded. On this day crossed on foot one of the water courses before mentioned. It was very wide, with then only about eighteen inches water. The north side was a perpendicular bank, about twenty feet high. The south was for many miles a level sandy plain, and cultivated in such a way as led me to believe that at some period of the year the country for miles round must be under water. Here we were met by a mandarin and a few soldiers. He had a paper in his hand, and as we passed called out our numbers, and was answered or corrected as the case might be. I here remember that as we entered one of the villages we were met by a procession of men, bearing each a bamboo branch, and some with flags, and in the centre was a handsome chair gilt, in which was seated a bamboo joss. The chair had eight bearers; I suppose it had something to do with joss pigeon. About mid-day we were halted for at least an hour and a half in the hot sun, and separated into two parties, and then started. I was taken to the left and the captain to the right from this halting place to Ty-wan-foo, which was about a mile and a half, and the land on each side was covered with graves, a few with the usual Chinese *tumuli*. The ground was very much broken up. Just previous to arriving at the gates we got a sight of the sea, but the other parties got a much better view, and observed a small low island off the town we entered, the east gate of which was in good repair, and the walls on each side for some distance had been whitewashed, but it did not prevent me from seeing a breach about a quarter of a mile to the northward. This face of the wall could be easily scaled, as from the broken state of the ground and the shrubs and trees which are scattered about, an enemy might approach within a few yards under cover. The gate and walls were like all others I have seen in China, and two large guns were placed in the gateway. I supposed both this and the white-wash was only for us to see how well they were prepared for war. After passing a short distance through a street, we came to a sort of open ground very much broken, with numbers of lofty trees growing, and with courses with stone bridges. Passing through this, we again entered among buildings, but we were not taken through any principal street, and after passing along some narrow lanes formed by the back premises, we emerged opposite a mandarin's house, and after sitting there for some time in the chair, which was nearly pulled to pieces by the people crowding to get a view at us, we were taken on a little further to another mandarin house, and then ordered to get out. We were marched inside the outer gate, and told to remain under the usual covering to Chinese gateways, where our tickets were copied; at least they began to do so, but the crowd soon became so annoying, both to ourselves and the mandarins, that the latter were glad to use their tails as whips, and then took us into a little joss-house on the right, where a man, who I think was a Chinese prisoner, was smoking opium. After remaining here some time, we were taken out again, but not before the door had been nearly smashed in by the mob two or three times. We were then taken back about 200 yards to the place where the chairs were first put down. We walked the whole way with the leg irons on, which cut my legs at every step; we were then taken to our present place of confinement, on the right hand side of the river yard of a mandarin's residence.

25th.—Captain Denham was examined as to the names, ages, wages, and duties of every body on board. (See Captain Denham's Journal of this date: post.)

On the 4th and 5th he was examined again. I met him at bluebutton's where he was examined, but I was not. Captain Denham was examined again on the 9th, when he learnt that both the shroff and carpenter had both been licked. The former had been telling the mandarins some yarns about Sir H. Pottinger, and from that time to the present Captain Denham has suspected him of having sold us. In the beginning of this month, I was up before the mandarin once, and asked my age, &c., and before bluebutton once, and no questions asked. From that time to this they have appeared to shirk me altogether for some reason or other, for although two of my fellow-prisoners, Mr. Partridge, and the gunner, have been frequently up before them, I never have.* During this month I suffered greatly, from fever, occasioned, I suppose, from want of air, and when the fever left me about the end of the month, I was attacked by piles, a disease I never had before. We never had a chance of sending a letter away, but Captain Denham made several attempts, in one of which he succeeded. Captain Denham was examined often, and was employed in drawing ships, an amusement as well as profit. Their party were much better off than ours (my usual luck), and it was not till May that I could get paper to recommence a log. Our jailer I believe to be the most wicked brute that ever was created. We were in a den so small that not one of us could stretch our legs at night, being coiled up like dogs. During the time I had the piles, I did not sleep for nights together. Ten of us, viz., the five sea-cunnies, two Manilla men, the gunner, Mr. Partridge, and myself, with a bucket in a wretched hovel only eleven feet six inches by seven feet six, and for two months and more we were confined in it, and never allowed out but once a day to wash, and at first this was not allowed, and when it was, for upwards of a

* This probably arose from the circumstance of Mr. Gully having no office on board the ship. The Chinese do not seem to have any idea of a class of men existing without official or other employment. The gunner (as already explained) was evidently considered a man of authority and importance.

month, only one or two could wash every morning, unless they washed in the water used by the others, the villain of a jailer being too lazy to furnish more than a few pints every morning. We soon found that nothing was to be gained by submission, so I took the opportunity one day of telling the rascal to go out of the place; he had come in to sky-lark with the sea-cunnies. He gave me a shove, and I sent him flying into the bucket. There was a great noise made about it, but nothing done. This now frightened some of my fellow-prisoners, but I followed it up by throwing the lamp at the second jailer's head a few weeks afterwards, and when I came back from Captain Denham's cabin in the beginning of June, greater liberty was allowed us. On our first arrival we found we were all more or less infested with vermin, and being so crowded, notwithstanding all our efforts we did not get rid of them, until Mr. Partridge, the gunner, and myself were moved into a separate place, and then the rest were too lazy, or at any rate they did not get rid of them. I arrived on this island in better health than I ever remember enjoying out of England, and a few weeks brought me down to a useless wretched being, disgusted with myself. The captain's party was better off altogether from being with or under a higher mandarin and having a more decent jailer. I have, perhaps, suffered more than any one, because I think I can safely say I have not had five days without sickness since my arrival. Not so with my two companions for they have not had as many days sickness between them.

In the examinations the mandarins always insisted that the Anne was a ship of war until Captain Denham went to redbutton's.* Their questions on other subjects related to all sorts of things, politics, size of men-of-war, complement, queen and court, and geography. They often asked who was the highest lotier here, and made a great fuss about putting down the names of the admiral, general, and plenipo, for they could not pronounce them. I may here jot down my view of our course of proceedings in leaving the wreck, &c. That it was the best course for saving the property I have no doubt, because it was the only one. Had we remained by the wreck we must at last have given ourselves up without a chance of saving any thing except the clothes we had on. By taking the earliest opportunity of seizing a junk as we did, there was a chance of our being able, if the weather moderated, to save some of the property by taking the junk round outside, and with that to retreat upon, we might have returned to the brig, and kept the rascals at bay until we could get the treasure &c., on board the junk, but with no prospect of escape it would have been folly to have fired a shot.

* Called the Toti Tygin, believed to be the senior civil mandarin on the island.

Commencement of Regular Log during Imprisonment at Ty-wan-foo.

26th.—Told by Jack that we are to be sent away in 120 days; but he did not know where. No signs of dividing us. Very wretched; one miserable day following another. No books; in fact no amusement at all to relieve the dreadful monotony of the prison; and worse than all no exercise.

27th.—Fine. Marched through the streets, legs and hands in irons, to Captain Denham's lotier. After a little while my hand-irons were taken off, paper and pencils put before me, and I was told to draw. I told them I could not. They then brought me a piece of paper with a strange imitation of a locomotive engine and carriages, by which I guessed that Captain Denham had told the people that I could draw a railway; so I commenced, and sent for Captain Denham, who confirmed my surmises.

June 9th.—I remained up to this date at Captain Denham's prison, drawing a few hours every day. In all I made about thirteen coaches of different descriptions, and a tunnel, all of which astonished the natives. During the whole time I saw nothing of the mandarin, except when passing through the room; and one day when Captain Denham walked out of the prison and got an interview with the mandarin to complain of his food, Mr. Roope and I followed. He promised to redress the grievance; but poor Quat, our jailer, a very good fellow, got fifty cuts over his thighs for letting us out. On the 31st of May, when we were drawing, a big junk-man, who took a letter on the 10th of April to convey to Amoy, returned with an answer from Captain Forbes of the Kelpie, giving us hopes of release, and other news. The man returned on the 4th instant, and took charge of another letter for Captain Forbes. Time at Captain Denham's prison passes much pleasanter and faster than here, and they have much more room. This morning I was taken up before Gee Sam y at, the lotier's head man, and politely requested to return to this hole, which I declined until the mandarin promised to ask the big lotier to allow me to live there altogether. I was then brought here in a sedan, after taking leave of all my friends. I don't believe a word of his promise, but intend to get back by some means or other. Find all here well; and allowed a little more liberty; viz., to wash in the yard, and no limit to the water.

11th.—Wrote to Denham, and sent it by Heen, the one-eyed man. This day, fifty cash served out to each person, and the executioner's room given up to the gunner, Partridge, and self. We cleaned it out; and such a mass of filth and dirt I never saw: without any exaggeration, I believe it had not been cleaned out for years. How the two men could live in it I do not know. We there had five blankets and mats to sleep on, and glad I am to get it. The lotier likewise gave us more than enough roast pork for dinner. During the day the gates of this place were shut, and quantities of chow-chow things carried. I rather think to-day or to-morrow must be the emperor's birthday, or some other great day.

12th.—Fine. We learn from Jack that there is to be a fête to-day. Several Chinese prisoners taken away from the opposite yard under a guard. One mace served out to each man, and Jack busy cooking all sorts of sweets. He says all the people of Tywan to-day eat rice boiled in sugar and saw-shee, and made into a kind of stickjaw. My finger still bad and under a poultice.

21st.—When dinner was brought to us to-day, there was an unusually small quantity of pork, half-boiled cabbage, and cheese made from beans. I was awfully hungry, but none of this could I touch, so I kicked up a row, and hove it into the yard. None of the nobs were at home at the time, but they shortly arrived, and we had a most laughable scene: first the fat jailer came, then the tailor, cook, and lastly, that scoundrel Gee Sam y at. I threw a piece of cabbage at the norhua, and told him to go and attend to his sewing; he then made off. Gee Sam y at flared up in first-rate style, because I told him if the lotier could not give us better food to let me go to Captain Denham's lotier. He was in a perfect rage, but only got well laughed at. It ended in his ordering other food for the morrow morning, and the fat jailer gave us 30 cash to buy cakes. This relieved the monotony of the imprisonment. The mandarin's attendant likewise brought us some cakes, after we had turned in. We evidently got the better of Gee Sam y at, for he lost his temper.

June 26.—Fine morning; gunner busy with brig during the day; had a touch of rheumatism. A row with the old rascal of a jailer, who was drunk and used dirty language. He got the worst of the row and the worst of the inquiries. The lotier heard us, and I believe talked of flogging me. Let him try it. Heen arrived in the afternoon with a letter from Captain Denham. I gave him one in return. He told us that Captain Denham was very sick. I trust he exaggerated, but shall be uneasy until I hear from him again.

27th.—Up early and boiled pot for tea; kept awake by a boil under my arm; did not get to sleep till past four. Wrote to Captain Denham. When breakfast came there was so little fish, that we all refused to eat any thing, except the gunner, who eat his rice, and Tow chin. The fat jailer came after a long time, and gave us some sweet potatoes and promised to speak to the mandarin and ask for more. This seems to be the mangoe season at this island.

They seem to be very good, and sell at the rate of 1500 and 2000 for a dollar. Captain Denham's lotier paid us a visit in state this evening, and all the attendants say that Mr. Partridge and I are going to see Captain Denham to-morrow: I hope it is true.

28th.—Fine. Had a good treat of mangoes. Nothing particular. Finished painting a steamer and line of battle ship attacking a French fort. No news.

29th.—Up as usual; fine morning. Added a little to letter to Captain Denham. Forty cash served out to each of us to buy towels. I suppose they have just found out that we might want such things. At dusk a prisoner was taken before the lotier, and they thrashed him and tortured him for two hours. He was flogged six times. Washed and holy-stoned the planks. A few hard showers during the day; otherwise fine. Nearly finished another picture, but spoiled it by reason of the paper running.

30th.—Fine morning; mosquitoes very annoying all night, and the mong hoon and light went out. No signs of going to Captain Denham. The man who was flogged last night received eighty blows in all. His crime is either forging or clipping of dollars. This day there was a large assembly of mandarins here, and the fellow was brought up again and tortured, not thrashed, for we could hear his cries for many hours, but no blows were struck. About 7 p.m., he was taken out for the purpose of showing where something was stowed, but I could not make out what it was; they found out what it was, however. Warm day. Finished a small picture of two line of battle ships, a frigate and steamer attacking a battery, and began the elephants for old Goa's friend. Received an order for a picture of the capture of Amoy.

July 1st.—Fine. Up as usual. Here is another month. Oh dear! oh dear! The gunner has taken it into his head that it is beneath him to draw pictures for sale; therefore will not partake of some of the things bought with the money obtained in that way. He is a fool. A man never lowers himself by earning his own victuals or even a few luxuries by the work of his hands, and to be consistent he ought to take nothing but what the mandarins give him. He is a Yankee, and therefore must be excused such folly.

2d.—Fine morning. Mangoes. Up as usual. Finished the large picture for the Pautow, who came and took it away. Flush of cash; consequently the mangoes, which are superb, suffer. They certainly assist in passing away the time. Commenced picture of Amoy, and another of a bear hunt. The latter for Heen, but I don't know when it will be finished. In the afternoon that big brute, José Maria, struck the boy who runs errands for us, in the loins. The lad spit blood for some time, then went away, and from what I can make out from the Chinese, fainted. The jailers, &c. all told us that he was dead. I knew better, but said nothing, as I thought a good fright would do the big coward good. The lad's father and the doctor came, and if the lad dies while José Maria is here, he will lose his head I have no doubt.

3d.—Fine morning. Mangoes. Up as usual. The last three or four days have been very hot. I suppose this and the next will be hot months. Nothing particular done about the boy. A new man sent here in the evening to assist the reilau in looking after us. Christened him Sam. Getting anxious for Heen.

4th.—A cloudy morning. Up as usual. More mangoes. I am afraid I ate too many as I was troubled in the morning. After breakfast we were told that the boy was dead, and that we were all to go before the great mandarin. It turned out to be a falsehood, and only Mr. Partridge and the gunner went to bluebutton's, where there were four mandarins, one a crystal button, with four gongs. They only asked some geographical questions ; *e.g.*, whether America had ever been in England, or if a man could walk from London to America in a week. If London was as large as America. How large London was? and what foreign possessions the English had. The captain and Mr. Roope were there. The captain quite well. They had a good meal at bluebuttons, and then a row with the mandarins because they would not let Captain Denham pay me a visit, and because we were so badly fed. It ended in their promising us more food, and also that Captain Denham should see me to-morrow. When Mr. Partridge and the gunner were returning, a mace was served out for each of us here. The shroff, who is evidently a villain in the interest of the mandarins, says that there has been a promotion here for taking us, and that they believe me to be some great man. They asked if Sir H. Pottinger was a white man or a *black* gentleman? Finished a picture of an engagement between a two-decker and a steamer. Quat brought us a present of mangoes. One of the understrappers said we were going away. Captain Denham and Mr. Roope are allowed a mace per day, and find themselves in every thing, since they came to their present habitation. The sea-cunnies behaved very badly, got drunk, hove their clothes out into the yard, and so misconducted themselves that the mandarins were going to put them into cages. They have promised to behave better, and are now in their place with no jailer at all. Sent my letter to Captain Denham. In the evening Heen came and brought a letter from the captain dated the 27th ult. Wrote him a short chit telling him that I had sent him a set of chessmen by Quat. Aticoa says the boy is still very ill.

5th.—Cloudy and hard showers with lightning. Up as usual. Mangoes. Fine days. The boy came back very ill, and instead of the brute who struck him asking after him, he and his friends blackguarded him, and tried to prevent his coming into the place. This put me up, and I flared up and tried to shame them. They held their peace, and the boy came in, and afterwards showed more good feeling than José Maria deserved, and more than ever I expected to find in a Chinaman. The breakfast was the same as usual, and we all refused to eat it except the Yankee who could not go without. I had the breakfast served out, and pitched mine into the yard. In the evening we got better fish, and Aticoa gave us a good supper of oysters and vermicelli.

6th.—Up as usual. Mangoes. Hard rain during the night and cloudy morning. Wrote to Captain Denham and then to the lotier, gave the production to Gee Sam y at, who came afterwards and promised us to speak to the lotier for better food for us or to send us to Quan. He brought me five sheets of paper, and wants something drawn. Hard squalls and rain during the day. Another boil on my skin —very painful—nothing done for it—food at night very short. Lewis broke his basin: no notice taken of it.

7th.—Up as usual. Hard rain and squalls during the night. It has come through the old roof. Mangoes. Cloudy morning and squalls of rain and wind during the whole day. No better or more food; so in the morning I commenced operations by heaving my basin and trash into the yard, and then smashing my bucket and sending it to look after the basin. Our abode afloat all day from the rain. Buckets of water pouring down in divers places. The gunner's picture all spoiled. Worse on the opposite side in the other prison. In the evening food the same; eat it and asked for more, but was refused, so smashed the dish, and Mr. Partridge walked up to the mandarin unknown to me and the mandarin promised more food and that the roof should be repaired, and that when the rain was over he would give us more money. I don't believe a word of it. At night the fat jailer came, and looked at the effect of the rain for the twentieth time and allowed two of our opposite neighbours to sleep on the tailor's bed. This day one of the cooks told us that a ship had been here but went away when the gale came on.

8th.—Hard rain during the night, with thunder and lightning. The surf has been heard during the last few days very plain. The last week we have felt the heat a good deal. Up as usual, but no mangoes; they don't do me any good. Hard rain nearly all day. We are told that there is another vessel wrecked: Aticoa is our authority, but knows no particulars. All hands promise us better food and more of it when the rain is over. Not able to get on with the picture of Amoy; the weather is too damp; consequently the day seems long and dreary. Aticoa says the vessel is wrecked at Tamsin Khelan, and that all hands were drowned. In the evening we had abundance to eat; and now I hope we shall go on quiet.

9th.—Up as usual. Am afraid of dysentery. No mangoes. Added to letter to Captain Denham.—Troubled with nightmare during the night; all stomach, I suppose: attribute it as much to the wet weather as any thing else. Cloudy, rainy, damp morning. Yesterday the sun was only visible for a few minutes, and then it was eclipsed I think. Strangers are not allowed to come and see us; that coupled with the report about ships may be something. At the evening meal the grub diminishing. A set of thieving, lying, longtailed rascals. Eat two pieces of rhubarb at night.

10th.—Rhubarb at work at five bells. Up as usual: fine morning. If I hear nothing from Macao to-day, I shall give up our friends there as good for nothing, unless some accident has happened. Cash getting very low. Fine warm day, but could do nothing in the artist line, so troubled with looseness in the bowels. Am afraid I am going to be very sick; every thing passes off like water; and yet I have a good appetite, good pulse, and no heat about the bowels. Still there must be something wrong, for my face is as white as a sheet, tongue and mouth foul, and I am called upon from twenty to thirty times in twenty-four hours. In the evening Heen came and brought two letters from the sea-cunnies, but none from Captain Denham, which is pleasant. Sent a letter to Captain Denham. Rather better this evening.

11th. — Up as usual. Still troubled with this complaint, and awoke with a severe pain a little below my right arm-pit. Fine morning: cool. Begun another letter to Captain Denham before breakfast. Mr. Partridge and the gunner were sent for, to go to some mandarins. Malwa came with Gee Sam y at, and gave me a piece of opium, which I swallowed to stop my complaint, and in a quarter of an hour it began to make me feel quite happy, in an hour quite sick, and laid me on my back the whole day. About twelve o'clock four of the sea-cunnies were sent for, and made to take their shirts with them: this, coupled with the appearance shortly afterwards of some soldiers with their matchlocks and baggage packed up for a journey, made me expect that they had taken the others out in small parties, on purpose to be able to remove us all to some other town. It is very odd the effect opium has upon me: I could not get up, nor could I go to sleep, but was in a sort of dream all day. Among other things it came into my head to apply to the East India Company, on getting out of this, for compensation as an officer of the Nemesis. About five o'clock my anxiety about our destination for another place was relieved by the return of all the party in good spirits, and praising the lotier they had been to. He is a clear redbutton man, said to be a Canton man; did not require them to go on their knees or to sit down before him. There was another lotier with him with a clear white button. The redbutton had a peacock's feather in his cap. The questions asked were much more sensible than former ones; and the mandarin seemed to have some small knowledge of geography. He seemed very much astonished that the queen had but one husband; of course I agree with him, and think it a hard case. He asked if we had written to Amoy, and on being answered in the negative, gave a kind of wink to the other mandarin; and when asked if he would like us to write, he gave no answer. He promised that I should go and see him to-morrow; and when he had prepared a place for us, that Mr. Partridge, Captain Denham, Mr. Roope, the gunner, and myself, should go and live at his place. He asked if we wanted any thing; and on being told that this was the queen's eldest child's No. 1 day, he sent for money, and gave the captain, Mr. Roope, Mr. Partridge, the gunner, carpenter, and myself, five mace each, and the sea-cunnies three each. A very good dinner was served, and when they were dismissed he made the usual Chinese salutation. Captain Denham was employed all day making him a chart of the world. All this is so very different from the conduct of the other mandarins, and so much more civil, that I am nearly certain they have either received a communication from Captain Smith, at Amoy, concerning us, or have heard some news from Pekin; and this is corroborated in a letter I received this evening from Captain Denham, in which he says that his mandarin sent him a message, to say, that he liked the English very much in general, and was pleased with him in particular. Mr. Roope sent his log for me to copy. Some of the lascars were up before the great man, and he eyed them with great curiosity. They were dressed in shirts and trousers which had been given to them; and the lotier seemed quite astonished to see our party without shirts, and promised to give them each one: he also gave each a fan. An attempt made in the evening to do us out of ten cash worth of tobacco, but it was defeated.

12th.—Fine morning. Much better, but got very little sleep; kept awake as usual with me, by the opium; and about three sticks I was awoke by Isidore, who was catting in great style and singing out with pain. After some time and talk the old thief of a jailer opened their door, and Louis came over and told me of it, and requested some tea. Mr. Partridge and I roused up, and in about a quarter of an hour or twenty minutes at most, gave Isidore a dose of rhubarb and a basin of tea. I slept little after this. Up as usual and wrote this. We had a slight shower at about four sticks. Here have two fine days passed and nothing done to the roof. Captain Denham agrees with me that it is very odd we don't hear from our friends. By-the-by all paper has been taken away from those at Quan's, and 150 cash paid for each picture begun. The excuse was that Quan was afraid it would get to the redbutton's ears that they drew English ships, &c. This of course is a lie. It is done to prevent them writing to Amoy. After breakfast a hard shower or two. About 11 o'clock Mr. Partridge and the gunner sent for to go to redbutton's, and about three in the afternoon they sent for me. I saw Mr. Roope, and after waiting outside about an hour, was taken before the mandarins. A white button, blue button, and our man, Mr. Partridge, the captain, shroff and mestry were there, all sitting before a fine large plate of light dumplings, which on my arrival were attacked with great impetuosity. Having finished them, Captain Denham commenced explaining a chart of the world he had spread before him. The lotiers making passing remarks upon every thing we did. One fellow said I was a Holau, but wanted to know why I had a hole in my breeches. I showed him one in my shirt. All our names were then taken down for new clothes, which are promised of a superior cut and make, with shoes and stockings to match. Several questions were asked about the Queen and Prince Albert, and they did not seem to understand about the queen going out when she pleased; indeed they cannot comprehend how we can have a woman on the throne. Asked about her dress, &c. About five o'clock we were dismissed and dinner brought us, which was tolerably good, but I would sooner dine at the prison, for I don't like standing to my meals with a parcel of riff-raff crowding round me. Gave Captain Denham my letter, and got one in return from him. The mestry says that an answer will come from the emperor in half a moon concerning us, and that if he orders our decapitation it will be done directly. This I don't believe. I find by Mr. Roope's log, that it is his opinion that the junk man did not take the last letter, which is a bad job, for our people over the water will not be aware of the Nerbudda's crew being here. Captain Denham thinks with me that the authorities here have had letters from Amoy concerning us. My being allowed to see the captain to-day, looks as if the redbutton was accustomed to keep his word. If so, we shall all go to live with him. Mr. Roope, I think, is a great deal too sharp tempered with Captain Denham, and does not understand a joke. He ought to show a better example, and he has always got some churchyard yarn or other about cutting off heads for his own annoyance and my amusement. He meets trouble half way, and is always looking at the dark side of the picture. I trust I shall be able to get to live with the captain.

I am not at all surprised at his having the blue devils.

13th.—Up earlier than usual; slept well last night. Fine cool morning. Wrote log, &c. Finished Amoy. Rain during the greater part of the afternoon. Some of our opposite neighbours have been amusing themselves drawing dirty pictures on the outside prison wall; this is pleasant. Dull day; no news. I think if it had not been for the rain we should have gone to some of the mandarins. As it is I dare say we shall not go until our new clothes are finished. The mestry asked me yesterday when we got out, if the English would take care of his wife and family.

19th.—Up as usual. Cloudy squally morning, with a strong gale from N. and E., and rain at times. Bowels I think are better, but am not certain whether it is the effect of the mango, the diet, or the N.E. wind, but think the last. About eight o'clock the wind began to draw round to the south, with hard squalls and heavy rain. About ten or eleven it blew a severe gale, and I have no doubt it is a typhoon down at Macao or Hongkong; but we don't feel it much here, being enclosed by buildings, and I am afraid that very little damage will be done to Tywan, the houses are so low. The water rose about a foot in the mandarin's yard. Our place was flooded from there being nothing to keep the rain out of it, which during the heavy puffs entered in torrents. We were obliged to crowd against the back wall to keep ourselves a little dry. Through the crevices of our planks we could see pools of water, and our planks were two-thirds wet. The roof likewise leaked in a dozen places. Our opposite neighbours quite as bad off, and I fear the captain will be worse. Nothing to be done all day because of the weather. In the afternoon it moderated, say about three o'clock. The wind about S.W. with heavy rain. It still blew heavy in puffs until about 3 p.m., when it died away after frequent puffs. On turning in we were obliged to crowd as close as possible, and then I was sleeping on damp planks. Pleasant for a sick man. I wish some of our friends over the water, who seem so coldly slack in their motions, could come and try a week of my life. They would be a little more active in our behalf, I think, or at least send us proper food and stores after it.

20th.—Up as usual; bowels same as yesterday. Dark cloudy morning. Cool day, with passing squalls of rain throughout. Employed on journal. Gave Aticoa the picture of Amoy. From Heen not making his appearance I suspect he has been frightened by reason of Denham's lotier having taken all the writing materials away. I am not surprised at it, but am very sorry, for we shall get no more letters from Captain Denham, nor be able to send any. The mandarin paid our opposite neighbours a visit this morning to look at the effect of the typhoon; it having blown one of the walls of the prison down, and killed a Chinaman. Some of the coolies of the establishment have been employed during three days carrying guns, so I suppose the fellows are still fortifying. I begin to think that we shall not get out of this at all, or at any rate not before next January. I shall give it up altogether unless I hear something by the 1st of next month. It is disgraceful. Only three days sail from Macao and one from Amoy. Perhaps they have been doing something, but I hardly think the Chinese could keep it so very close. At dinner there was so little beef that I sent it back, and the dish was filled in a proper manner without a word.

21st.—Beautiful morning. Getting better, I hope. Saw soldiers going out with rusty spears, and afterwards the rusty weapons in the yard were brushed up. Fine day, but warm. The typhoon has all but destroyed the mangoes. Employed on journal. Wrote to Captain Denham. In the evening some poor devils were taken before our mandarin and tortured; we could hear their cries quite plain. Unless we hear something before the 10th proximo, I shall die of disgust.

22d.—Fine morning; up as usual. The lotier out very early before daylight. He returned after breakfast and went over to the Bengalees' prison, I suppose to see how the bricklayers are getting on with the repairs of the wall which was blown down. Better to-day. Nothing doing and every thing particularly quiet until the evening, when they brought us for dinner a few prawns, which I sent back, and they then gave us the usual dish of fish. After this some Chinese came and gave all hands some cash, but José Maria, who was last, happening to get one less than the rest, the great booby threw them away, and walked about for half an hour, uttering all sorts of maledictions, much to my amusement. He managed to fix the quarrel upon José Dias. I am heartily tired of these fellows. They do nothing but grumble and quarrel among themselves, William Norris excepted.

23d.—Up as usual. Fair morning; dreamed all night; nothing but nightmare. Beautiful day; but no sooner had I nearly got rid of my bowel-complaint, than I am attacked by the piles or something of that sort, which lays me on my back all day. I was rather better at night. The clothes which we were measured for the other day we now hear we are not to have until the cold weather comes; and although they have repeatedly promised for nearly two months to have the roof of our prison mended, they have given no signs of commencing. They never speak the truth.

24th. Fine morning. Any thing but well. Beautiful day but cool. About 8 a.m. Captain Denham's lotier came with another, bringing the shroff and mestry with them. The Nerbudda's people were taken before them and examined as to their ages and names. This, after having been twelve months on the island, is rather good. I had a few words with the mestry who said that John Williams and another lascar of the brig's crew were dead, and that the remainder were allowed to run about the town, because Captain Denham told the lotier that they would all die, unless allowed to go about in the sun. My boy is very well, and very anxious to come and live with me. If we go to redbutton's, perhaps I may be able to manage it. Here he would be useless. Mr. Partridge told the mestry to tell the mandarins he wanted to speak to them, so after they had finished, he was sent for and asked what he wanted. He said that we had not received the clothes which had been promised us, and that we were all getting sick, and wanted to be allowed to walk about in the yard. They answered that we (three of us) were going to redbutton's in five or six days. That they had received the order, and that when we went there we should get our clothes, which were not then finished. They then laughed at him and he came away. There may be truth in it, but I cannot place much credit on it. Added to Captain Denham's letter. Piles very bad all day. Our boy who runs errands, a few days ago commenced smoking opium, and in consequence experienced all those agreeable symptoms which boys in England have on beginning to smoke tobacco. From this we may judge to what extent the smoking is carried. Indeed from what I have seen, I doubt if ninety-nine out of every hundred who can afford to spend 30 cash a day, do not use the drug in simply eating it. I can buy enough of the eating drug to make me drunk, for less than 10 cash. This day, while on my back, devising all sorts of places to conceal my log if shifted to red-button's.

25th.—Up as usual. Fine morning, but slept badly. Nightmare all night. I have just thought that in case this should survive us it may be interesting to know the furniture of our abode. The cell is all but as large as the opposite one from which we were removed. but we have three advantages over our opposite neighbours, viz., 1. There are only three of us. 2. The window has only single bars. 3. We have air-holes in the roof. To sleep on we have five hard-wood planks about eight feet long by fourteen inches wide and two thick. The floor is of broken bricks. A bamboo is slung nearly the length of the place, on which in the daytime we hang our mats, two in number, for sleeping on. Besides these I now see two towels hanging from it, one made from part of an old pair of cotton drawers, and the other of grass cloth given me by Zu Quang Leon. Ditto belonging to Mr. Partridge, and a bundle of papers, sketches, &c., tied up by a string. On the east wall are the remains of a picture of Chin Hoe damaged by the rain. The window faces the west. On one side of it is hanging my pipe, given me by the captain's party. On the other is a small looking-glass given me by one of the jailers, a number of pencils and four monghoons. Our pillows of pieces of bamboo, with a qunny-mat for keeping the afternoon's sun out of the place, and a checquer-board are on the planks On the north wall are hanging our washing-tub, which cost us 50 cash, a broom for sweeping the planks, a basket containing some hooks, &c., belonging to the former occupants; a basket containing our chop-sticks and spoons of bamboo, the gunner's towel and a stick for carrying a lantern. In this wall is a small recess containing a clay lamp and stand, a few bamboo sticks, and two iron wires for cleaning pipes, three papers of tobacco and some waste-paper. In the corner two sticks have been driven into the wall, on which rest the logbooks and some papers. Below that is a small shelf, on which are placed several cups, and broken saucers, and paints, two chow-chow cups (I broke the third a week ago), given us by Jack, a small earthenware kettle for boiling tea-water and brewing samshu when we can get it, given us by Aticoa. Below the shelf is suspended a hollow piece of bamboo holding our firepan, and below that a small fireplace, likewise a present from Aticoa, a cooking pot bought by ourselves, another containing charcoal (the pot given by Jack), several old straw shoes and pieces of bamboo for smoking out the mosquitoes. On the south side are pendant, 1st. the Bank, a string of cash about 80 or 90, a fan, a small basket containing a few opium pills and our stock of tea, my hat which cost 30 cash; I have covered it with oiled paper. I am sitting on a bamboo stool which belongs to the former occupiers of the place, my foot resting on another given Mr. Partridge by the towka (I suppose the head jailer). Opposite is the door, behind it the bucket; on my left is the window, on the sill of which are two combs, one of which I bought for thirteen cash a few days after my arrival at this town, being money I had saved from the mace per day allowed us during the journey. My fan is sticking in the window, and I am writing with this book resting on a board painted red with black characters on it, and two green eyes above looking at them. I think this is all. No, I have forgotten to mention that on the south wall hang my long ell trousers given me by Kitchil, lascar, my grass cloth ones, given me by the lotier, and a pair of woollen socks given me by Francis; and from the same string hangs Mr. Roope's log. If you can call any thing in this list a luxury, you must recollect that we have only had it lately; for two months we had nothing, and were annoyed by myriads of fleas, bugs, lice, ants, musquitoes, and centipedes, without a possibility of getting rid of them, except by death or a miracle. I have on my back now the only shirt (and a woollen one too) I have had for nearly five months, and half a pair of cotton drawers are on my legs. I omitted to mention, that on the north wall is my calendar. Every morning I scratch with the head of a rusty nail, the day of the month. We have also a third wooden stool lent to us by Aticoa. Employed we are, but the days are awfully tedious, and I am sadly at a loss for something to pass away the time, and feel the want of books.

26th.—Up as usual: fine morning. Short of cash; no bread to my tea; no supper last night; and no prospect of getting any. At last they have commenced repairing our roof, and we have in consequence been in a nice mess all day; but it assisted to pass the time away. Washed the blankets. Mandarins employed at bluebutton's trying prisoners.

27th.—Up as usual: beautiful morning. For the last three nights I have suffered from the nightmare: in the first night I was in a ship, looking out for Chapel Island in the English Channel, when we got among the rollers, and I never was in such a fright while awake: the second night I was a real personage in the Miller and his Men, convinced that I was to have my throat cut: last night it was something about Macao, but I forget what: I suppose it arises from the stomach and want of exercise. Received a short chit from Captain Denham, by our mandarin's pipebearer. Captain Denham's lotier is absent somewhere, and our fellow is doing duty for him. Captain Denham has been told the same yarn about a house being furnished for us. He is unwell again: he has given Heen two cattees for me, which I have not received. Gave the pipe-bearer a small packet for Denham, and wrote another, in case of Heen's arrival. Very warm day. In the afternoon Heen came into the yard, and sat down on a stool a short time by the old man. He then came over to our gate, and the boy opened it for him, and immediately went over to the head-jailer's place with the excuse of bringing him some tea: the old man's son was in our outer yard. When the tea was brought and drunk, Heen asked for a pipe, and came inside, followed by the old man's son, and I then saw that he was suspected; so I returned into my den, and put my letter away, determined that it should not be my fault if he was found out, and I kept aloof during his stay. While lighting his pipe he endeavoured to give a chit to one of the sea-cunnies, but failed; and the boy, who just returned at the time, as well as the old man's son, both saw it. In a few minutes the head-jailer came and sat down inside until Heen went away. Heen behaved very well; and after coming inside saw that he was watched, so did not try any more; indeed it would have been folly to have done so. When he went out the head-jailer followed, and said something to him. I was very glad to see him go through the gates, for I fully expected to see him seized every minute and searched.

From the quarrels and rows there were afterwards, I doubt if he is yet safe: however, it is not my fault: I told him before always to stuff the letters into a cake, which, if he had done, he would have never been discovered. They were evidently on the look-out for him, and suspected something from his first arrival; and as this is the first time he has been since the captain was at Redbutton's, I dare say they think he is the channel of communication with Amoy. Won't I take the first opportunity of paying our jailers for this. Rain in the evening.

29th.—Up as usual: dull morning: surf very plain all night. The mice have taken away Captain Denham's letter. Wrote to Captain Denham, but am afraid we shall not have a chance of sending it. Rain and squalls throughout the day. Last night prisoners were brought in, said to be the Tamsin rebels, thirty-five in number. This tallies with the yarn told Captain Denham about that part of the island being in a state of rebellion. Captain Denham has been told by somebody that we are to be given up when all the places which the English have taken are restored; and that we are to be well treated; and I have now made up my mind that we are not to get out of this till January, and shall therefore make strong efforts to get to live with the captain. Having observed, for some time, a reluctance and sulkiness about serving the food out among our opposite neighbours at meal-time:

I asked this morning Lewis about it, and it came out that they said they had observed me call one of the jailers to look how much he gave himself, which was the reason they would not serve it out. Of course this was all a lie, and I told them so in plain language; for I was disgusted at their believing me guilty of such an action; and determined from that moment to have nothing more to say to them; and at the evening meal made the jailer bring our food into the prison. Within the last week or so the cooks have shown a disposition to improve our food, which has been met by the sea-cunnies by all sorts of growling. Now three of us can mess aloof, and keep ourselves free from all these rows. The fact is, the food lately has been much better than they ever got on board the ship, for a continuance; and it would serve them right if the Chinese returned to the tittlebats and greens again. Our jailer short of cash, and trying to be very civil; but by the Lord, if I catch him tripping! Commenced a regular walking exercise; did about two miles and a quarter. By-the-by, the gunner knew the cause of the sulkiness over the way a week ago, and never said any thing. He is a curious man.

30th.—Up as usual. Thick rainy morning, with fresh breeze from N.E. Surf still very distinct. Did not get to sleep before three sticks last night, and then dreamed I was with the general, taking towns, &c. Cloudy and overcast day, with fresh breeze from N.W., and squalls throughout the whole day. The head jailer sends us a plate of sweet potatoes in addition to each meal. The pipe-bearer won't even look this way: I suspect he does not like the risk of taking letters. I can't blame him, and shall not press the matter. The bricklayers have done little or no good to our roof. The holan told us we are going to redbutton's, when the rain and wind are over. I wish to God we could get anywhere out of this place; for I am disgusted more and more every day. Accomplished nearly four miles of exercise this day.

August 1st.—Dull dark morning; up as usual. Finished the other volume of Log, and commenced this. Very warm. Slept well last night. Alternate showers and sunshine, with light squalls throughout the day. Late in the afternoon some of the redbuttons men came, and Mr. Partridge and the gunner were taken away to Quan's, where they were joined by Mr. Roope, and proceeded to redbutton's. At first a few questions were asked them concerning the chart which the captain had drawn, and they had pasted on a large sheet of thick paper the passages to Indian ports, marked in red ink. The shroff, as usual, had a great deal to say; and among other things told the redbutton that the English had no factory at Canton now. What the devil does he mean. After this Mr. Roope was asked why he had been kicking up a row at Quan's. He said that Captain Denham had been dangerously ill, and would die unless removed to a better place of abode, and reminded redbutton of his promise that we five should live together at his place. He was answered that the gale of wind had blown down the commencement of the building, but that it would be finished in a few days, and then we should go. Mr. Roope then requested that I might be allowed to see Captain Denham. The redbutton pointed to the gunner, and seemed to have made some mistake between gunner and Gully. Mr. Roope told him that he had not seen me. He then promised that I should see Captain Denham to-morrow. Mr. Partridge and the gunner were then taken to Quan's office to see Captain Denham, and they found him looking very ill, but he was a little better than he had been. Mr. Roope said he had been so ill that he did not expect him to live. I am afraid that if he has any more attacks in the wretched damp hole in which he is, that it will bring him very near death's door. At present I don't think there is any danger, and if we could get to live together, that his health would improve. Mr. Roope sent us two mace and Chu Sam y ats gave us one. Mr. Partridge and the gunner then went to see the sea-cunnies, who were all well, and their place looking very clean. They saw my boy and the lascars who have got a good place for exercise, and all have had clothes given them. They have good grub and are allowed four cash a day each, so that all hands are better treated than ourselves here. Indeed from all accounts our mandarin is a great brute, and the short time he was doing duty for Quan was awfully severe with the criminals, and sent two with their right hands all blackened over, to the redbutton for his approval of the sentence, which was to have the hands cut off. I did not hear the crime. Quat, who up to a late period had been jailer to the captain, and was a great favourite when I was there, had been behaving so badly altogether of late, and had robbed them twice, that Mr. Roope complained to the mandarin, who licked him well, and they do not know what has now become of him. The last time he had robbed them of thirteen mace, and brought back two dollars, which he offered to Mr. Roope; he had been gambling, I suppose. They now have an old man who cooks for them, and Chu Sam y ats acts as their banker. Mr. Partridge and the gunner returned about nine o'clock. While they were away the man who took them came back and told every body that the redbutton had given them money. This was evidently done to cause a disturbance with the sea-cunnies. I do not know why, but on thinking over the circumstances, I am of opinion that the junior mandarins have some reason for keeping me away from the redbutton, and seem to shun me altogether. That villain of a shroff has been telling them some lie or other. It is my luck. I am getting heartily tired out. Until within the last week I have contrived to keep my spirits up better than most of the others, but I am now done up, and I really think have lost all pluck. The captain's illness and the non-receipt of the expected letter from Amoy I suppose to be the cause, coupled with the disappointment of living with the captain. I must try and keep up, I suppose; God help me. As to going to-morrow to Quan's, I don't believe a word of it, any more than I believe we are going to live together at redbutton's.

2d.—Dull morning with hard showers; clearing up about 11 a.m. Washed planks. Up as usual, passed a very bad night. My companions observed lots of singsong pigeon, and the redbutton has another mandarin next door licking prisoners during their examination. I got yesterday, per Mr. Roope, a letter from Francis, who amusingly enough begs me to have the goodness "*to take him out of this infernal prison.*" I wish I could, poor boy, or myself either. He gives a sad account of the sickness of the lascars. The captain has been told the same yarn by Quan that we were by Sam y ats, viz. that we were to go to the redbutton's in ten days. Walked five miles yesterday; upwards of four to-day, and washed planks. While taking my exercise in the yard to-day, a man came to the gate and made a noise like a pig. Mr. Partridge was sitting on the stool outside, and remarked to me that "he had thrown a piece of crockery ware for me to tread on" (I had no shoes on). I was vexed at this and stooped down to pick up the crockery to throw at him again, when I found it to be a paper with something inside it. I looked up at the man and immediately recognised him as the same man who took Captain Denham's letter when I was at Quan's. When I could examine it without being observed, I did so, and found it contained five cash, and was written on as follows: "The bearer brought Captain Denham's letter, he and his brother are pilots." It was signed Duncan Forbes, and dated 14th May; the same date, I think, as Captain Forbes's letter. I can only suppose, from these circumstances, that Mr. Roope's conjecture is right, and that the man has lost Captain Denham's second letter to Amoy, is afraid to return to Quan's for another, and has come here for one. I immediately wrote one, and we shall be on the look out for him. I trust he will return for it. It turned out a fine day, but I was not taken to see the captain according to promise. In the evening Aticoa told us we were positively going to redbutton's in three days. He said the mandarins had said so; therefore I don't believe it, and I would rather now remain here a little longer, to give the junkman a chance.

3d.—Very heavy rain during the night, and our roof leaking as bad as ever. Up as usual. A dull rainy morning. Rewrote my letter to Captain Forbes. Wrote to Captain Denham informing him of the appearance of the junkman. The boy came in suddenly and saw me folding Denham's letter, but I don't think he said any thing. He is rather afraid of me. Yesterday evening and this morning the old jailer swearing like fury. He is short of cash, knows we have some and will not give him a chance of stealing any. In my letter to Captain Forbes, have told him of our wretched situation, of the captain's health, imprisonment of the Nerbudda's men, want of medicine, suspicion of shroff, lies of mandarins, death of lascars, &c. About 11 a.m., while playing draughts with Mr. Partridge (the rain having driven all the others inside), the junkman came to the gates. The old man was luckily out selling baskets, the young man drunk with opium, and the boy playing draughts inside. I beckoned him, without moving, to go to our gate, which he immediately did, and Mr. Partridge did the same. Teug was outside his door. The man went right up to Aticoa's room, called in Teng, gave him some betel and told him he was going to have a ship drawn by the monna's people. He slipped out, gave a piece of paper, and received the letter to Captain Forbes. I only said 100 dollars; he said "how, how," made signs that he was off in a junk, and away he went, and delighted I was to see him go. Not a soul had the least suspicion. I then told the sea-cunnies of it, and gave them instructions how to act if I am absent and the answer comes. So far so good, and

I have no doubt we are under the special care of providence, for had we gone as we intended, to live with Captain Denham we should have missed this, perhaps, the only opportunity that may occur of communicating with Amoy, so whatever may happen now I shall think it to be for the best. A nasty drizzly rainy day; it prevented me walking more than four miles and a quarter, but could not damp my spirits. The mandarin was not out all day. Added the good news to the letter to Captain Denham.

4th.—Hard rain throughout the night. Slept well, but dreamed of being shipwrecked twice and burnt out of a ship once. Saw two dead friends. Was going to a ball at Greenwich, and from there to the highlands. What can possibly be the cause of this. I always wake with a dead weight at my chest. Up as usual, a dark rainy morning, and seeing the mandarin going out has suggested to me that it may be interesting to any person into whose hands this may fall to know something of his establishment, as it proves that he must have perquisites as well as his regular salary, which we are told is only 100 dollars a month. His head-servant, Sam y ats, a sort of secretary; two clerks under him, Kin-twya, Ayung-twya, and another, name unknown; two tailors. These are in-door servants. Palee, the man who sings out to the out-door servants the mandarin's orders, and receives chops, chits, and cards. Kin Siung ya, a man who repeats his orders personally to whomsoever they may be sent; he also is *supposed* to keep the court clean. Five palanquin-bearers, four of whom carry the palanquin, and one the umbrella. Four men with *comical conical* caps, who sing out and carry rattans. Four police runners. A man in front who delivers the mandarin's card, and his pipe-bearer who walks by the side of the palanquin. Besides these, there are, I think, two in-door coolies and one "sa" who lives outside. Of their pay I can say nothing certain. The palanquin-bearers, at least one (Aticoa) gets eight dollars per month. There are also living in the house two young men who appear to be completing their education, as a schoolmaster comes every morning, and several other pupils with him, and they leave in the evening. Independent of all these are the cooks and jailers, women servants (if any), and a barber, who comes every morning to shave the mandarin and dress his wife or wives' hair. (This, by his own account.) Jailers, we have an old man, his son, and a boy about fourteen years of age; over the opposite side live the cooks, the principal jailers, with the Bengalese and Chinese prisoners. The Towka and a quiet old man have the superintendence of all. To show how universal is the use of opium, I need only say that all the above whom I have had the opportunity of noticing smoke opium, with the exception of one boy who lived with us some time, and left because he could not agree with the old man. He is now doing duty over the way. I have marked with a cross all those I have seen smoking or cleaning their pipes.* They all say that the mandarin smokes. I am sorry to say I think another custom is also very common, from what Aticoa told me about the boy here, and from what Captain Denham observed in his former prison. It is considered disgraceful, but not with the abhorrence and disgust it justly merits in our country, and I doubt if it is in the list of the punishable crimes. I have omitted to mention above, a little good-tempered girl about ten years old, named Ko-ne-o, who runs about the court, and is a great favourite with every body. She often stops to have a chat with Mr. Partridge. This and a little baby, who delights me by dirtying the dresses of every body who tries to pet it (and they are many), are the mandarin's children. The two scholars are said to mess with the mandarin. In addition to the above, concerning opium smoking, when I was at the captain's prison, it was there practised morning, noon, and night, from the boy about fourteen years of age, to the old gate-keeper. Rain all day. Walked five miles.

5th.—Heavy rain all night. Ditto morning, up as usual, dreamed I was at Macao, at A. J——'s,

* The tailors, Palee, the palanquin-bearers, the rattan men, the cooks, the old man, his son, and the boy.

who told me I was 3000 dollars richer than when I went to Tyman. I hope it may prove true. A very uncomfortable morning before daylight. Painful tightness about my chest. I suppose this rain will put off our going to redbutton's; I suppose it is all for the best. Warm day with a few light showers. The boy's father here all day smoking opium with the old man. Took his son's clothes out of pawn where the old thief had put them, and bought opium with the money. In the afternoon Partridge saw Quat coming to the great gates. He beckoned him, and asked if he would take a letter, but as we were giving it to him the old man sent him away. He loitered about the gates, and we made the chit fast to a brick and threw it to him, telling him to take it to Newman. He picked it up and off he went.

Here the journal of Mr. Gully ends. He had got to the end of a little paper book which he had made, and it would seem as if he then possessed no means of continuing his diary. In all probability the refusal to allow him to draw pictures for the Chinese had deprived him of the opportunity of secreting for his own use a little of the paper furnished him for drawing. He afterwards seems to have obtained one single leaf, and a new journal appears to have been begun on the very day on which he was murdered. He was perhaps interrupted in the act of beginning it and led away to death, for he has only written these words, "1843, Aug. 10; Attempted to boil water without fire, but curiously enough failed!" He had made a calendar on a small piece of paper, having written in the figures from the 13th of May to November the 10th inclusive. Each day appears to have been blotted out as it passed away, and in this calendar the 9th of August is the last day so blotted. The 10th is wholly unmarked.

The annexed diagram is a fac-simile of the calendar.

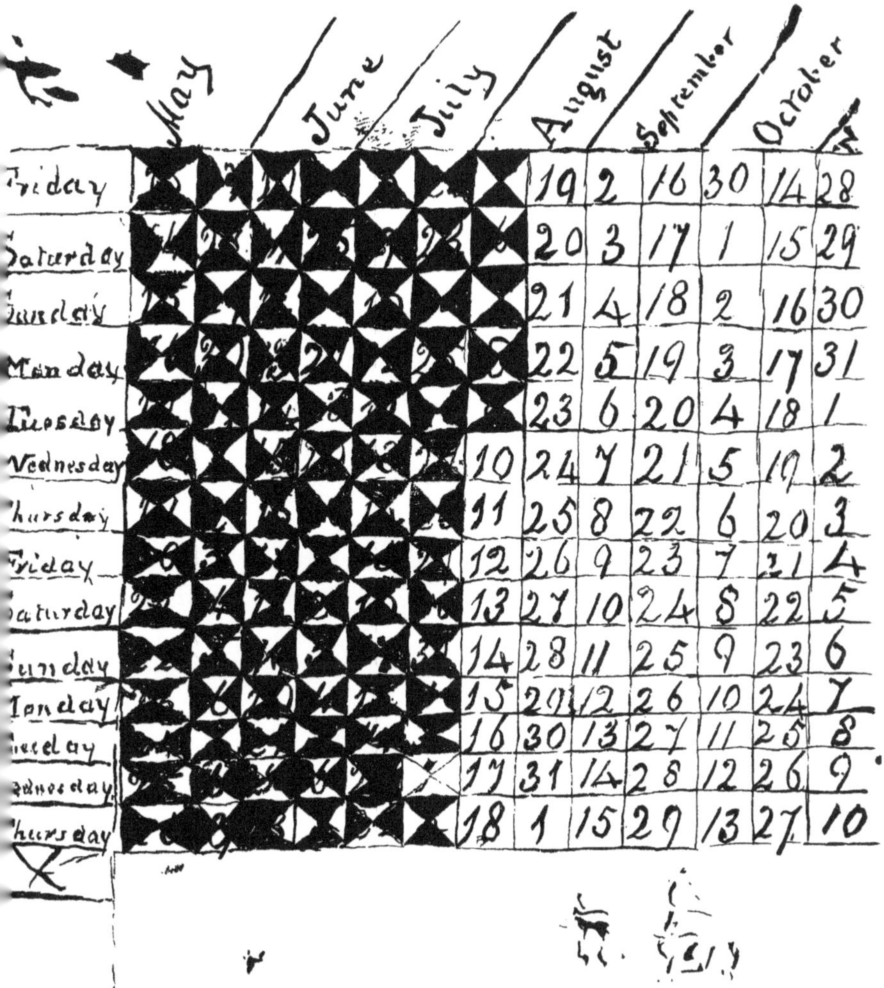

Friday		19	2	16	30	14	28
Saturday		20	3	17	1	15	29
Sunday		21	4	18	2	16	30
Monday		22	5	19	3	17	31
Tuesday		23	6	20	4	18	1
Wednesday	10	24	7	21	5	19	2
Thursday	11	25	8	22	6	20	3
Friday	12	26	9	23	7	21	4
Saturday	13	27	10	24	8	22	5
Sunday	14	28	11	25	9	23	6
Monday	15	29	12	26	10	24	7
Tuesday	16	30	13	27	11	25	8
Wednesday	17	31	14	28	12	26	9
Thursday	18	1	15	29	13	27	10

Note. — The 3 of August was blotted out with red, all the rest with black paint.

JOURNAL

KEPT

BY CAPTAIN DENHAM.*

March 8th.—Light northerly winds and fine weather. At 10 a.m. we weighed in the brig Anne from the inner anchorage or Chusan harbour, having on board R. Gully, Esq. and servant. Passengers 2; self, 2 officers, and gunner 4; sea-cunnies (Europeans) 10; 6 Chinese (carpenters, shroffs, and servants) 6; and 35 natives of India (lascars) 35; in all 57 British subjects. At 11 passed through the Sarah Gally passage, and stood towards Keetow Point. Falling calm used our sweeps, and at 4. 30. p.m. anchored under Keetow Point. Night calm and cloudy.

9th.—Daylight, light north-easterly winds and light rain. Weighed and sailed through Goff's passage, at the southern entrance of which, fell in with the

* Such parts only of Captain Denham's journal have been retained, as do not describe matters already described by Mr. Gully.

barque Arun and schooner Lynx ; received some letters from the latter, and anchored under St. Andrew's Island, for the purpose of receiving treasure from her on freight. At eleven, having finished transhipping, weighed and stood to the southward. Towards noon the breeze freshened, and off the Quesan Islands we exchanged colours with an English ship bound to the northward, supposed her to be the Hoogly, daily expected. After passing Shippo, hauled in, intending to anchor for the night in Sammoon Bay, but the wind keeping fresh and steady, determined to make the best of my way to Macao, touching at the ports of Chin Chew, Amoy, &c. At sunset, the Heysan, or Black Islands bore east from us, and from them I took my departure; the south extreme of land, bore at this time south by east, distant about ten miles southward, south by east half east till eight o'clock, then south till ten, and after that south-south-west, being the direction of the line of coast, which is very little known, and has many islands a long way off shore—position not ascertained, and many not down in any chart. During the night the breeze increased considerably, and by daylight was blowing a fresh gale, with thick rain and a heavy sea running.

10th.—Continued strong north-east wind, with thick rainy weather. At eight a.m., steered south-west, keeping a good look out for land but saw none. Noon to sunset, ditto wind and weather.

Shortened sail at six p.m. to the topsails and jib, keeping the same course. At eight, squally, with continued rain, lowered the topsails on the cap, and steered south-south-west. At ten, in first reefs, still keeping the sails on the cap; continued thick rain. At 11. 30, squally, with hard rain, sent the crew aloft to take in the second reefs, intending to heave-to till daylight, and being by account twelve or fifteen miles to the north-east of Ockseu, and fearful I should run past Chin Chew during the night, worked up the dead reckoning carefully; indeed, this I did every four hours, and allowed one mile and a half per hour, south-east current. Mr. Gully more than once asked me if I was not steering too much to the westward. The fore topsail was soon reefed, and I had sent the gunner forward to spill the after-yards, the men not being able to reef the sail in consequence of the strength of the wind, and it being nearly aft. While in the act of doing this, a man aloft sang out "Land on the larboard bow:" put the helm down immediately when he again sung out "Land on the starboard bow." The vessel immediately struck about midships on a reef. We could see nothing from the deck, the night being one of the darkest I think I ever experienced, together with thick rain; the breakers could neither be seen nor heard till we were on the reef. Clewed up the topsails as soon as possible, the sea breaking clean over us, and taking every thing moveable with it, and forging the brig further on the reef. About two minutes after we struck, a very heavy sea struck her, taking her completely over the reef, and tearing the rudder-wheel, which broke in two pieces, and with it broke the stern-post. The wind was now on the larboard quarter and the brig fell on her larboard side, the sea almost staving the decks in. Kept the masts up, in the hopes they would help to lay her over on her starboard bilge, which, after one or two seas striking her, she did: we immediately cut them both away, and commenced clearing the long-boat. On taking off the hatches to get her masts and sails up, found the hold full of water, and the water-casks floating in the hold: sent immediately to get the powder and magazines up, but found them completely damaged. The tide now began to leave us, the bulwarks along the starboard side were nearly all gone: the quarter-boat, binnacle, and loose spars, and in fact every thing that could be washed away, was; and it was with the greatest difficulty that any one could hold on: the chief and third mates, and some lascars, were washed from their hold, but fortunately succeeded in getting a gripe of the main rigging. Till now I had thought we were on one of the Samyets, but the rain holding up a bit, I saw the low land close-to, and feared we were on Formosa. The tide leaving us fast the vessel was quite easy, and I now saw that her stern frame was entirely gone: I determined to wait till daylight and see where we were, and see what chance there was of being able to send the long-boat to procure us assistance, and if possible save the freight of treasure we had on board; the cutter was unfortunately stove by the fall of the foremast, and the other boat, as before mentioned, washed away.

The powder, as well as all the cartridges were damaged: we turned to, to make musket cartridges, with some fine powder I had, and what we could pick out from the damaged: at this we worked till near daylight, making in all about four cartridges for each musket: some of the rest of the people were employed putting food, water, compasses, and sails, &c., in the long-boat; after this I made all the people put on the best clothes they could get, giving my own, the officers and Mr. Gully doing the same, many of them put on two, and some three shirts, and Guernsey frocks.

March 11th.—At daydawn continued strong gale, and being low water the brig was high and dry. A Chinese came down to the beach, when the carpenter was sent to ask him the name of this place, and get what information he could. The man was very frightened and ran away. We got him at last but could make nothing of him. As the day broke found we were on Formosa. I then called all hands together, and told them my determination to leave the wreck, and try if we could not get possession of some small junks, the mast-heads of which we could just see as the light increased, begging them all to keep close together, and not straggle. As soon as it was well daylight we saw the quarter-boat and loose spars nearly a quarter of a mile from us. The brig was on a shingly beach, with black sand and several straggling rocks. Outside of us, on a line with the beach, was a long reef as far as we could see, and which we must have been forced over. Fortunately when we struck it was high water spring tides; had it been half or quarter ebb every one on board must have perished. It was also impossible to get the long-boat out through the reef, there not being the smallest gap in the long line of rocks over which the sea was breaking very high and violently —it would have been madness to attempt it. Thus situated, our only chance of saving our lives appeared to be in getting on board the Chinese boats, and trying to get over to the main land. I was fearful also that the vessel would go to pieces, as the tide coming in, and the wind and sea increasing, rendered our remaining in the wreck very dangerous; (this proved afterwards to be the case, as either twenty-five or twenty-eight Chinese were drowned in her that tide, as I heard some time afterwards). Accordingly, all agreeing with me, we started about seven a.m., with nothing but our arms, a few extra clothes, and a sextant, chart epitome, and spy-glass. I again gave particular orders not to straggle, but keep close together. We commenced our march over a sandy plain to the north-eastward, where we had seen the boats. There were many fresh water streams, which we crossed about knee deep, and more inland we saw here and there a few straggling huts. Making the best of our way for the boats, about eight or half-past eight we came up to the creek in which they were. It was very narrow, about fifty feet at low water; they were all aground. When they saw us they beckoned us to come on board, which we did, the water not being much above our knees: they were at chow chow. Myself, Mr. Gully, officers, and about half the men, went into the largest junk, the remainder of the people went to the one close astern of her. I believe there were four or five junks in all, but all very small, the largest I should say about fifty tons; they were also deeply laden with rice and ground nuts. The wind was blowing directly into the creek, off the mouth of which was a continuation of (I suppose) the same reef we struck on. Our only chance now was a shift of wind, for had even the breeze moderated and continued as it was we could not get out of the creek till the sea went down, unless blessed with a change of wind.

I now got the carpenter to explain to the junk-men that if they would take us to Chin Chew or Chimoi I would pay them 3000 dollars. He said he could not say, as his master was on shore, but that they were going to Chin Chew in a day or two, or as soon as the wind moderated. He told us to wait and he would tell us by and by, but that at present we could not get out of the creek. This was too true, and all of us saw our chance of escape at present hopeless. To add to our miseries it now began to rain, and we were as close as we could stow in the junk. I now learnt that two of our party, the principal shroff and one lascar, in consequence of straggling, had been seized by the Chinese, who were mustering in strong parties, and hundreds were hastening to the wreck. I sent the chief mate with the best ten men I could pick out to see if he could not get them ; but he very prudently shortly after returned in consequence of the numerous bodies of armed natives who were advancing towards us from all quarters. The North shore was completely covered with men, all armed with spears, matchlocks, and long knives, many with shields. The junk was now afloat (10. 30. a.m.), but in consequence of the heavy wind we could do nothing but submit to our fate. I saw plainly there was nothing for us but imprisonment, perhaps death. To avert the latter I would not allow a single shot to be fired. Shortly after, two decent looking men beckoned us to go on shore. This we declined doing, hoping the breeze might moderate or shift, and give us the slightest chance of escape. Finding we refused to go on shore they went away. They were attended by a large body of soldiers, and most of those collected on the beach were soldiers, with their jackets turned inside out to hide their uniform; I should say there were about 500 men within ten yards of us. For some time they contented themselves with using very threatening gestures. At last they began stoning us, and very soon demolished the mat covering over the junk. This annoyed the junk-men very much ; they wished us to fire on them, but I would not allow it. They also attempted to cut the junks' cables, which were on shore. One fellow in particular was very active, but the junk-man pointed a musket at him whenever he went near the hawser, and again begged me to shoot him; but I again declined, and had the greatest difficulty in preventing some of my people from firing who had been struck by the stones ; seeing no chance of being able to get the junk out of the creek, it would have been madness to commence hostilities, especially as we had not more than four rounds of cartridges each. We could certainly have killed many of them; and had we had plenty of ammunition, I should have stuck out to the last; had we fired all we had away, they could have stoned us out of the junk, or at low water set fire to her. I therefore determined to wait and trust to chance for our deliverance. We did not give ourselves up, as from the gestures of these savages we could expect nothing but instant death. The rain now descended in torrents, and they went behind a kind of sand-bank to one or two huts, and some sheds, about sixty yards off, and commenced firing some matchlocks; but I think merely for the purpose of intimidating us—at least such we conjectured.

In the afternoon the tide falling rapidly, they again made their appearance, joined by a mandarin in a chair, and another body of soldiers; the mandarin shortly went away to about half a mile distance, where the chair put down, and there he stopped. Shortly after this they came on board two or three at a time, till the junk was quite full, when the rest made a rush, and I then gave up all the arms we had, expecting that we should be taken prisoners as we stood; but no sooner were they in possession of the arms, than they commenced stripping us in the most brutal manner, with their knives drawn, and threatening to murder us. We were knocked down, and almost every rag taken from us; my cap and shoes, with a refinement of cruelty, they tore off and pitched overboard; many of us were as naked as we were born; they left me with a part of a Guernsey frock, and a small part of a pair of drawers; every one in this junk suffered the same, lascars, sea-cunnies, and all, with the exception of the Chinese shroff and carpenter. It was intensely cold, and blowing a strong N.E. gale, with heavy rain; we tried to get into the junk's cabin, but at every attempt were struck over the hands and feet, and driven from our purpose. After they had stripped us, they started off, and made a signal with a handkerchief on a spear, which was answered by the mandarin's party, who immediately advanced, and pretended to be very active in dispersing the wretches who were running off with their plunder in all directions. He then beckoned us down, and the junk-men getting sticks, knives, &c. to drive us out of the junk, we gave ourselves up; and thus naked, cold, and weary, were given in charge of three or four soldiers to each of us. Our party in the other junk were not stripped, they did not even board her. We now commenced our wretched march, or rather run, for they kept us on a kind of trot, the wind and rain continuing. I never felt the cold so bitter; we suffered greatly in our feet, having no shoes on; and our route being over a beach, covered with rugged shingle, broken shells of all kinds, our feet were consequently cut severely at every step, and our route might be traced by the blood; it was horrid, and even now makes me shudder, and wonder we did not drop on the road. We passed close to the unfortunate brig, and for miles the scene of plunder was most wretched, the ground covered with all kinds of boxes, chests of drawers, casks, and in fact, every description of article the imagination can picture; the vessel, at least what remained of it, was swarming with soldiers, and parties were running in all directions with the ill-gotten spoil. I turned to go on board for the purpose of getting hold of any thing that would cover me, but was knocked down by one of my guard, and almost stunned by a blow on the head from the butt-end of a spear. However, he brought me to my feet and senses by applying the point, and threatening by gestures to run me through if I did not start on. I did so as well as I could, and followed the rest. We crossed several streams, and a few houses or huts here and there; at last about six, p. m. we crossed one larger than common, in which were several junks moored, the water was up to our middle ; on the opposite side was a small village, and here we were halted, and all of us who had arrived, were put into a sort of barn, full of paddy-husk. Glad were we of this bed, bad as it was. After begging a time, I got a drink of water, my tongue was so parched I could not speak. We very soon buried ourselves in the paddy, but it pricked us very much. In about an hour they brought us each a basin of warm congou, which was very acceptable; but we could get nothing in the shape of clothes. The distance we must have come, I should say, was about ten miles, bare foot and naked, and the coldest day I ever recollect in China. Many of our party were missing ; the officer's servant and ship's cook fell down dead on the road from cold and fatigue. William Norris, sea-cunny, was brought in in a basket, naked and senseless, and several others during the night in the same manner ; the wretches tumbled them out of the baskets like can of wood, and then left them to recover or perish. The rest missing, were the gunner and some sea-cunnies and lascars, about sixty, I think; these we heard were taken to some other place where a petty mandarin lived, and were better treated by some women who gave them some rags to cover themselves with (they being stark-naked), and some Chinese wine and bread or cakes. After our fatigue we very soon fell asleep, and painful to our skin as the paddy was, slept soundly all night.

15th.—We were here much too closely confined to even guess at the weather, but about noon were greatly rejoiced at seeing the gunner and his party arrive. They had been much better treated and had, as before mentioned, clothes given them; the latter of a kind that would under other circumstances have created a laugh. The gunner was dressed in a kind of kilt or petticoat, with a child's cap on his head; the rest much after the same fashion. The cause of this apparent kindness was I think on account of the gunner having a mermaid and other similar things pricked on both his arms, from which the Chinese thought, and indeed during the whole of our captivity continued to believe, he was a great man, but of what rank could not determine. Our food as yesterday.

17th.—We were all taken out this morning and placed before a bench of mandarins, and each as he passed had his tally taken from his neck. He was then handcuffed and one mace given. After this he was placed in an old chair, lashed on bamboos and taken out of the town according to his number under a guard of three or four soldiers, each man with a runner who had charge of the key of his prisoner's irons and his mace. We were preceded and followed by a small troop of cavalry, and in this way we were marched in a south south-westerly direction as near as I could judge by the sun, which was very powerful. The roads were very bad, and many of us encountered falls owing to the slippery state of the ground and the narrow pathways. We have observed that the regular soldiers were well armed; the matchlock being kept in good order, and apparently of a superior make to what any of us had seen used by the Chinese; many of them had the appearance of being rifles, the barrels being cut outside six square, and were very clean; most of them, however, were ragged, and armed with spear and sword, also the rattan shield, but they were universally dirty in their persons. The first part of this day's march we passed through cornfields, and the country was fairly though not highly cultivated, but the rice or paddy fields appear to be the best cultivated of any I have ever seen in China. In passing through these places we were abused and called all manner of names; our hair occasionally pulled by way of amusement; they also threw all sorts of filth at us, and the children, and often full-grown men spit at us as we were carried along: *the women were better behaved, and a few looked on us with much apparent sympathy*. They are, I think, the ugliest race of females I ever saw in China, owing perhaps to the constant chewing of the beetle-nut and chuman, which makes their teeth as black as ink, and when they open their mouths it is like a round black hole, neither teeth nor tongue being discernible, all being alike quite black; which contrasts strongly with the face, which in almost all classes, even the lowest, is painted or rather powdered white. They have almost all the small feet, but all appear to take great pains in dressing the hair; even women labouring in the fields have their heads dressed either with natural or artificial flowers, and all have earrings, even children in arms have this apparently indispensable ornament. At one of our halting-places a fellow swore I was a woman and insulted me. I gave him a blow that astonished him a little, and proved pretty plainly that I was not, at all events, one of the gentle sex. Being handcuffed he got the weight of both hands, and the benefit of the irons, which cut his lips very much. The bystanders appeared to enjoy this; for they all pointed at him as he got on his legs, and burst into shouts of laughter. The fellow went away swearing heartily: no doubt he would have retaliated but the soldiers prevented him. We saw to-day several carts of a very rude sort, the body made of bamboo wicker-work, and the wheels a large circular piece of wood. These were fixed to the axletree, which of course revolved with the wheels, the body of the cart being connected with this by large cleats in which the axletree worked.

About sunset we arrived at our halting-place, a large and densely populated town, with high red brick walls; there was a small hill close to it with a fort on it. For some miles before we arrived here the country was thickly covered with paddy-fields and swamps, with here and there small hamlets surrounded by trees, of which the bamboo was most conspicuous from its height and splendid foliage. In one part of our day's march we saw the mast-heads of a few small junks. On entering the town we were surrounded by the natives, who crowded round us in hundreds, spitting at us and behaving in a most brutal way; so much so, that it was quite a relief to get to our quarters, which I suppose were about the centre of the town, and were the common jail, in the middle of which were the stocks. The jail was built of wood and two sides of it were stout bars of the same material. To get to this wretched place we had to pass through several passages and doors, at each of which was a guard. We were stowed in two of these with a space about twelve feet square between us, and all round the yard were other similar dens full of the most miserable objects I ever saw in the shape of human nature. Soon after our arrival we had some rice and a sprinkling of salt greens; also some salt fish, but so little that any one who got a piece was considered fortunate. The fish was only the tails, fins, and snouts chopped up small, and I am certain there was not a quarter of an inch of this for each man. On the whole, during our stay here, the food was most abominable, and nothing but the pangs of hunger could have made us eat it.

18th.—Very cold, and to add to our miserable situation it rained all night, and continued to rain while we remained in this town; the roof of the prison leaking all over, kept us wet and cold. Before breakfast I was called for by the jailers and a Chinaman named Ayum (who had been many years ago a servant to a gentleman at Singapore, and had picked up a few words of Hindostannee), and by them taken out of the prison to a large court-house, where I saw three mandarins in state. On appearing before these officers I was made to kneel down, and saw close to me the carpenter and shroff, both kneeling, and resting with their hands on the ground. The mandarin then commenced his examination of me by asking what ship it was, and if I was the captain. I told him I was, and that the vessel was an American; this they appeared to know was an untruth, as it certainly was, and to prove to me the contrary, they showed me an English ensign, and had a board brought out with several flags painted on it, but I was too far off to distinguish them. Seeing the mistake I had made, I said immediately it was an English vessel, and that I was the captain or head man on board. I was then asked if it was not a ship of war? I answered no. How many guns we had, the quantity of powder, small-arms, and number of men, and many similar questions, all which I answered with strict truth. They then declared it was a ship of war, and on my again denying it I was threatened with torture, and a kind of frame brought in and placed before me; however I still stuck out. They then began flogging both the carpenter and shroff on the face with a leather flapper, consisting of four pieces of leather joined at the handle, and about the size of a palm of the hand, the ends about an inch apart. I was taken on one side after this, and told by the man Ayum that I must answer the mandarins' questions in a manner to please them, and that they would behave well to me; but if I did not, that I should be flogged and placed in the torture frame. I told him I would tell the truth and stick to it that the vessel was not a vessel of war, and if they liked they might kill me, but I would not answer them as they wished. He then went and spoke to the mandarin, who ordered me some breakfast, and I was taken out of irons, and had, such as it was, quite a hearty meal; they themselves going to their breakfast in an inner room. I was crowded with people, and could hardly get a bit of air, so great was their curiosity to see me eat. On the return of the mandarins I was taken again before them and placed on my knees. Shortly after one of them, on my asking, allowed me to sit down; this was a great relief, as the other posture was most painful. They then commenced a series of questions, and finding Mr. Ayum was humbugging and telling lies (his knowledge of the language being confined to a few words), I requested the carpenter might act as interpreter, which, after a deal of bother, was allowed. Having asked and received all the answers regarding the vessel, they began a series of questions that would puzzle any one to recollect. They were very particular about the Queen; how many husbands she had, and who Prince Albert was; how many children they had; and many of their questions were of so indelicate a nature, that I told the carpenter I could not answer them; in fact no person would believe the gross (and frequently absurd) questions asked, and these by the government officers and men of rank. They brought some charts and a piece of newspaper, out of which I was ordered to read to them. This I did, of course much to their edification. They then asked about the war, and who the principals or mandarins were, taking down their names. Then they wanted to know if the English were not afraid of the Chinese, and if I was not afraid. I told them that the English being then on their way to Pekin, did not look much like fear, and that I certainly was not afraid of them, because if they killed us the English would soon hear of it, and would come and burn all the towns on the island and kill all the troops. I was kept sitting here answering all their questions till about eight o'clock at night, when I was given some dinner, and afterwards taken in to where they were having theirs. One chap, after having picked and sucked the feet of a pig, gave them to me as a treat to finish. However, this I declined, and to my surprise was brought some from the dish, which was very good. They also gave me a cup of samshu, which I drank; this was the first time I ever tasted that liquor. They brought the brig's binnacle and compass, and questioned me till about 10 p.m., when I was dismissed, and heartily glad was I to get back, having been either sitting on the ground or on my knees, from seven in the morning. I wanted them to let me take some food to my unfortunate fellow-captives, but they would not allow it. During the day I asked them to let us have water to wash, not having had that luxury since the day of the wreck. They told me that it was against the laws, but gave me a basin of water to wash in, and a piece of dungru, about eight inches square, for a towel, and this was only allowed, in order that they might see how I washed myself. On my way back to prison, having been securely ironed, the carpenter and shroff said we should all have our heads cut off, that the mandarins were bad men—they had been licked over the face and back for not answering the questions as the mandarins wished them, and begged me to answer in a manner that would give the wretches satisfaction; in other words tell lies. This I refused to do. The mandarins would have it that the ship was a man-of-war, and had gone to Formosa to look after the crew of the "Nerbudda" transport, the crew of which ship (wrecked about last September) the people told us were still on the island. This we did not believe, but afterwards found out it was true. Right glad was I to join my fellow-prisoners, for I was tired, and in spite of the wet floor and clothes, slept soundly all night.

21st.—We resumed our journey this day, and arrived about sunset at another walled town, and were here confined in a large joss-house, which had been prepared for us; the floor being covered with straw, on which we slept very well, but the irons troubled us a great deal. Many of the people here managed to get their irons off, but I was not able to do the same. As soon as we were all settled down a scene of opium-smoking commenced. Every soldier had his pipe, which was carried openly and stuck in their belt like a knife. They made no hesitation of smoking before the mandarins, all of whom, I believe, use it more or less.

24th.—Early in the morning we again resumed our march. We had a route to-day over a more hilly tract of country, and a sort of lake we crossed, very large, but not more than twelve or fifteen inches deep, the upper end of which was very precipitous, and looked like the walls of a town; but on approaching found it was earth presenting a flat surface, and quite perpendicular, and about thirty or forty feet high: we had to go round to get at a gap in it, up which we were taken. We met a religious procession on the march, which to-day was shorter than our previous ones. About 2 p. m. we were all halted, but not allowed to get out of our chairs. Here we waited about one hour, when a mandarin and a company of soldiers came up with a list of us. Our numbers were then called over, and here we were separated, passing on in our turn. Mr. Gully, Partridge, the gunner, and seven men were taken into the town of Tywanfoo by a road to our left, and the rest of us entered it by a gate facing the sea. We were taken to a large court-house and placed on the ground, hundreds of people coming to look at us. The walls of this town, at the gate we entered, appeared to be in good repair, and about thirty feet high: we entered by the west gate, the other party by the east; there were several guns mounted facing the gates, and covered over with mats. The mandarins and followers had a deal of trouble in keeping the crowd away, or rather in trying so to do, so anxious were they to satisfy their curiosity. Finding they could not either drive or keep them off, we were separated into three parties, and put into three separate places of confinement: myself and eight others in a small den, the five Chinamen in another, and the Lascars in a third, but all belonging to the same establishment; in which places we were immediately locked up. At night we had some rice, a few greens, and rather more fish than usual. From the place we were wrecked, which was called Tamsia, to this town (Tywanfoo), we made seven marches, and the distance, as well as I could guess, about 130 to 140 miles, mostly in a S.S.W. direction. My fellow-prisoners were Mr. Roope, chief mate, five seacunnies, the chief mate's servant, and one lascar. Our prison was about seven feet by eight, with the bucket in one corner. At night we all laid down to rest, but I could not sleep; I did not like being separated from Mr. Gully and the rest of the Europeans.

25th.—I was taken out by myself, and walked to an inner court-house, where I was placed on my knees and examined by the head mandarin of this establishment, who, I afterwards found out was the Quan or mayor of this Foo or town. He asked me many questions about the wreck, and had our carpenter as interpreter, as I could not understand Ayum (the Chinaman who acted as interpreter). He would have it that the Ann was a ship of war; I of course persisted in her being a merchant vessel, and told him we were bound to Macao. To all these and many similar questions and answers, he told me I was a liar and a very bad man. After keeping me some time, I suppose for all his friends and dependants to stare at and satisfy their curiosity, I was sent back to prison. We had two meals a day all the time we were here, such as they were.

25th to 31st.—During these days we were crowded with visiters of all sorts, and at all hours, coming to see the "barbarians," many of whom spat at us through the bars of our place of confinement; we were each allowed a very small portion of tobacco daily, and had two small pipes among us. We were shockingly dirty, but were not allowed to wash; however, after a deal of entreaty, the jailer, after washing himself in a little warm water, feet and all, the same water being used when he had done by the under jailer or servant, we were allowed the benefit of by the latter dipping a dirty piece of cloth in it, and handing it through the bars for us to wipe our face with; but after a day or two he gave us the basin of water inside after they had both used it: but dirty as it was, it was a treat to us; at last we persuaded them to let us have clean cold water to wash in: they did this after some demur, wondering at it very much, as the Chinese all wash in warm water. I may here state that the old trousers I had, had become like all the rest, so covered with vermin, that I was glad to take them off and wear the bag around my middle. The prison was full of lice, fleas, bugs, rats, cockroaches, and centipedes; our situation was most wretched: the natives think nothing of vermin, I don't think there is a native on the island who is not covered with them, men, women, and children; and often have I seen them picking them from another's head and clothes, and destroying them in a way quite novel to us,—viz., by eating them. Strange to say, none of the Europeans got them in their heads, only on the body and clothes.

31st.—About seven o'clock this evening all of us who were on this establishment were taken up before Quan, with him were five other mandarins, only one of whom I had seen before, it was the same man that examined me at the town we halted at, and which I believe was called Carghee. I since found out that this man was called the took-too-low-yah, he wore a white transparent button and a peacock's feather. Quan, only a brass button. We were all placed on our knees before these officers; a more naked, wretched set of beings could scarce be seen, all of us with hands and feet in irons. Here all our names, ages, country, capacity on board, duty, wages, and such like questions, were asked, and on being answered, written down, our mandarin sent for a little bread, which was given to a few of us, I believe more to see how we ate than out of any compassion for us. About nine o'clock we were all taken back to our separate places of confinement and locked up. The carpenter told me he was in the same prison with the rest of our Chinamen, which was the condemned cell of the place; they, at least the five belonging to the "Ann," had a thin kind of red jacket on, this is a distinguishing mark, I believe, for traitors to their country.

April 4th.—This day I was again taken singly before Quan, who examined me again, regarding the names, wages, and duty of all hands on board, there was also a deal of cross-examination and trying to get me to say there were 100 and more men on board, but I stuck to the same story as before, in fact, it was the best, besides being the truth. Quan was very angry with me, and after remaining a long time in the presence of this fellow, was sent back to my den again.

6th.—To-day, shortly after our morning's meal, a guard of soldiers came into the yard, in front of our prison, and I was taken out, hands and feet in irons; on reaching the yard I was set on the ground, and a chain, about six or seven feet long put round my neck; thus ornamented, and almost naked, I was dragged through the town to a large court-house, when I was delighted to see Gully and the people who were in confinement with him,—viz., Mr. Partridge, third mate, the gunner, five sea-cunnies, and two lascars, natives of Manilla; shortly afterwards we were all taken to an inner court, and as usual placed on our knees before four mandarins, the principal one, to whom this establishment belonged, wearing a blue button and peacock's feather; his title we afterwards learnt was the Pwoon-hoo-tygin. Here the same examination took place, about the names, ages, country, &c., of Mr. Gully's party. After this was taken down in writing, all were sent outside except me. An examination similar to the former ones was again gone through with the same result, except that I was not called a liar; I begged hard of this man to give us clothes, and allow us more food, to all of which I was answered by saying it was China custom, and the emperor's orders. About nine at night I was dragged back, the leg irons hurting me very much, which as soon as I got in my prison, I broke or rather forced (with assistance from my fellow-sufferers) open and took off, the chain was taken off my neck, and a receipt given to the soldiers for me by the jailer, who then locked us up.

9th.—This morning, for the first time, we got pens, ink, and paper, the first I have had since our arrival here, and to-day I have commenced this journal, having to trust entirely to memory for the foregoing dates, there may be some mistakes regarding them, but as near as I recollect, they are correct, all other circumstances are true, and to the best of my memory, faithfully recorded. Of course we could only appropriate small pieces of paper, as it was given us to draw on, which we did, and gave drawings to the men who brought the paper, they promising to bring more paper, and some of them gave us a few cash. During the day I was had up before Quan, when I saw the carpenter and shroff; they had been telling some story or yarn about Sir H. Pottinger, for which they both got a licking, and I began to think the shroff was telling his own story to the satisfaction of the mandarin, and at the same time telling lies about the brig; and I was the more inclined to think this as the mandarin allowed him two mace a day from this time to purchase opium with, he being in the habit of using the drug, not a cash of this money did he give either of his four unfortunate companions. After a few unimportant questions about English ships, I was dismissed, and taken back to prison again; continued drawing ships, &c. the rest of the day.

10th.—To day, after a deal of coaxing, and entreaty, the jailer, to our surprise, allowed us to wash and clean our den out, and from the quantity of all sorts of filth we cleared, I should think it had never been touched since it was built. Otherwise continued drawing pictures, the demand increasing considerably. This evening a Chinaman came, and watching his opportunity, made me a sign that he would take a letter across to Amoy; in order to be less observed, he sent Aquat, the second jailer, out to buy something; the senior being engaged with his opium-pipe. I wrote a note, stating our present wretched situation, and promised the man 100 dollars on delivery.* He immediately secreted the letter, and shortly after the return of the second jailer he went away, cautioning us by signs to mention the circumstance to no one. I could sleep none that night; how fervently did I pray that the good fellow might succeed without being discovered! the penalty would have been the loss of his head. He was a Chinese sailor or junkman, and his brother was a pilot and fisherman, but I never saw the latter.

11th.—Employed all day drawing ships and different kinds of pictures for the natives, which we did for amusement and profit; nearly all the cash we got went for a kind of bread which was cheap, and, though abominable stuff, was, in our reduced and starving condition, quite a treat. This afternoon the man I had given the letter to came to the prison, and stood so that we could observe him; he then showed us the chit, inclosed in a piece of red paper, with Chinese characters on it, cautioning us by signs to be sure and not let the jailers know it, or he should be killed; he was obliged to be very cautious, making signs only when the jailers happened to be looking

* This letter was delivered. The copy of the *Canton Free Press* received in London Sept. 3, 1842, mentions the fact, and says that the letter describes the captives to have been "kept by the Chinese in four different prisons, not far from the sea side almost opposite to Chimoa, and very severely treated." It adds, "We hope that her Majesty's ships of war will be able to do something for their release."

another way. He gave us to understand that he was going that night, and when the jailer turned his back he put a piece of paper between our prison bars, on which he had drawn a fort, with an Englishman standing over the gate of it, firing a gun, and at the back all kinds of warlike implements; in the front he had drawn a Chinaman holding up a letter. It immediately struck me that he wanted to know whether the English would receive him kindly or fire at him. I directly scratched on a piece of paper a Chinaman giving a letter to an Englishman, and receiving from him money and other things; this I gave him when he again made his appearance in the evening, and I could see he understood me, as he gave me a nod, and hid the paper in his sleeve, starting off immediately.

13th.—Still drawing—plenty of visiters—all wanting pictures—some paying a few cash for them, others running off as soon as they got them, without payment. We were told that Ayum, the man who had been at Singapore, had been flogged; this I was not sorry for, as he was a noisy, lying rascal, making himself very busy, and at times telling me if I did not answer agreeably to the mandarin's wishes, he would get me a licking.

14th.—As usual employed drawing all day, and to the astonishment of the natives completed a three-decker; the questions asked about this, and the squabbling it created, caused a precious row: every body wanted it, but none could pay the price;

it was the largest that had yet been drawn, and the paper was about two feet square; at last a fellow bolted with it, but returned presently, bringing with him some bread, which hunger compelled us to take as payment.

17th.—During the day a barber came in to shave the jailers' heads, and the latter, wishing to see how we should look without long beards, whiskers, &c., asked us to be shaved; this we very readily agreed to; each had his face clean shaven for the first time since our misfortunes began, and for which each paid six cash; these cash were the profits of our labours in the drawing line, and at times we had a few given us by charitable people who came to see us, but these, I am sorry to say, were very few. It was not at all an uncommon thing for them to pretend to give us cash, and when our hands were out between the bars, to have some filth put in them, or else have them spit in.

18th.—This morning Mr. Roope and myself were taken before Quan, who told us he wanted some ships and pictures drawn, and that we must do them; we were then put on chairs before a small table, our irons taken off, and pens, ink, and paper given us: here we were employed till the afternoon, when we were put in irons and chains, and dragged away to the Pwoom-hoo's, when we met Mr. Partridge (3d mate) and the gunner, from whom I heard that poor Gully was unwell, complaining of fever. I was very anxious to see him, but this was impracticable; all I could do was to send him a message by Mr. Partridge. We found out to-day that Ayum, instead of being flogged, had been rewarded with a new suit of clothes, a cap, and a fan and case, by the mandarins; the latter he took every opportunity of displaying to an admiring gang of natives, telling them what service he had been to the mandarins, and in what a splendid way his services were rewarded: the brute also tried to frighten me with threats of decapitation, if I did not take care and answer the great man as he (Ayum) should suggest. Fortunately I saw the carpenter before I was taken to the inner court, and was enabled, in consequence of the vanity of Master Ayum, to slip a letter for the coast into his hand, which he managed to secrete unobserved. On being taken before the mandarins, I was of course placed on my knees, and an examination commenced relative to the power of her Majesty over her subjects. First, however, they inquired if England was governed by a man? I told them that the reigning sovereign of Great Britain was a lady, loved and greatly respected by her subjects. At this they all burst out laughing, and afterwards asked if she was married? I told them she was. They then asked now many husbands she had? I told them only one; and that by the laws of my country no woman could have more, and that a man could have only one wife; but that on the death of either, the survivor, be it man or woman, could again marry. This they seemed to think absurd; polygamy being allowable to men of any station in China; if they can support 100 women they may have them:* the priests and disciples of Bhudd are, however, vowed to celibacy. They then wanted to know if women had small feet in England? I told them they had, but naturally so; and that in no country but China were women's feet deformed. Then followed a series of questions regarding women in general, and her Majesty in particular, of too indelicate a nature to mention, and so very gross, that I refused to answer them, for which they threatened to lick me. However, finding I still refused, they at last burst out laughing, and shortly afterwards sent me back to prison ornamented as usual in chains and irons accompanied by our guards; I may as well say here, that we were never taken out of jail except by a written order, and always on our return, a receipt given by the jailer to the officer commanding our escort.

19th.—This morning our jailer was taken before Quan, and received fifty blows on the back of his bare thighs for allowing us to be shaved. He bellowed out most lustily, and when brought back, they got two eggs, the white of which they beat up in some cold water, making a thick froth which

* This is not quite in accordance with the statement of the Chinese laws made by Mr. Davis, who thinks that but one wife is allowed, but that the practice of having hand-maidens is, at least, tolerated.

they applied to the bruised parts; after this Mr. Roope and I were taken up to draw as yesterday, not a word was said to us, however, about getting shaved. In the afternoon I was taken to bluebutton's again, where I met Mr. Partridge, and the gunner; heard from them that poor Gully was still complaining. I was shortly taken in and placed on the ground, the pwoon-hoo was the only mandarin present, he was very busy writing, occasionally speaking to his pipebearer who was the only person present besides me. Here I was kept till about eight in the evening, during which time he did not once speak to or take the slightest notice of me. I was very tired, being kept so long on the ground, and could never make out why I was sent for, particularly as the carpenter was not there to interpret.

20th—Early this morning we were taken out to draw as before, and about noon taken as usual through the town to bluebutton's. About twenty of the most miserable looking Chinese convicts, ornamented like ourselves accompanied us as far as the outer door of the hall, when they were placed on the ground. We were taken to an inner court-house, where we saw Mr. Partridge and the gunner, and were much pleased to hear from them that Gully was quite well. Mr. Roope was also better, having taken the medicine: these three were, viz., Mr. Roope, Mr. Partridge, and gunner were taken in, and a few questions of no importance asked. I remained outside and was not examined to-day; they remained a very short time inside, and on their coming out again we were all taken to our respective places of confinement.

24th.—This morning I was taken up before Quan, where I saw the carpenter, who told me he had given my letter a to man who told him he was going to Amoy in four days, and that he would deliver it on receipt of 100 dollars, and promised to bring us an answer back for the like sum. When Quan came out I was placed before him and questioned about our year, the number of days, weeks, and months in it, how many festivals we had, and how we knew them, and how many of them there were annually appointed, &c. He then asked many questions about the sun, moon, stars. After answering all these, many of them most absurd, he ordered me some breakfast, which was very good, but very little of it. When I had finished I asked for more, in the vain hope they would comply, but I was marched back to prison again, but shortly after taken out to draw for Quan. Our food had now become so bad that at times, hungry as we were, we could not eat it, and this night our dinner was stinking; I kicked up a row with the man who brought it, and threatened to show it to the mandarin. He promised to bring better to-morrow, we were therefore obliged to make the best dinner we could of a little dry rice, an article of food I detest.

25th.—We had a better breakfast than usual.

This morning we heard that the head mandarin had arrived in this town, and that we should be taken to his place and be examined. Shortly after breakfast Mr. Roope and I were taken to Quan's and had a shirt and pair of trousers given us of coarse blue dungru made very small. When we had put them on we were chained and ironed, and then each placed in a kind of sedan chair and carried out guarded by soldiers, both horse and foot. We stopped at a large building where we were taken out of the chairs and led to an inner sort of yard. Here we saw Mr. Partridge and the gunner, who told me that Mr. Gully was not very well; they had both received and put on similar clothes to ours. After being almost smothered with people for about half an hour, we were taken into the great man's presence and placed on our knees, the chains were then laid along the ground, the end of them in a line with the mandarin; there were three other mandarins present. The principal one wore a transparent blue button, a peacock's feather, and a string of beads round his neck; after asking and taking down our names, all the others were taken out again, and they commenced their questions by asking the names of the head English mandarins in China; I told them Sir H. Pottinger, plenipo, Sir W. Parker, admiral, and Sir H. Gough, general; they took a long time getting these names put down on paper, and asked among numerous absurd questions, whether Sir H. Pottinger was a white or a black man, if he was a great mandarin, how tall he was, and what strength he had, how he was dressed, how many wives and children he possessed, and what were their names. I of course told them I was utterly ignorant of most of these things, but that he was the representative of the Queen of England; the same questions were asked about the admiral and general with the like insults. Then commenced their questions about the queen, her name, the name of her husband and children; and, in fact, so many absurd and ridiculous questions were asked that in any other situation, I should have enjoyed it much; they only asked me one or two indelicate ones, which, finding I refused to answer, returned to others. They wanted to know how the queen went out, and when she did if the people were allowed to look at her. I told them she frequently rode out, sometimes in a carriage, at other times on horseback; this was laughed at and disbelieved, but finding I persisted, they wanted to know if she sat astride. I told them no, and tried to explain; they then made me draw a lady's saddle on paper, to do which they took off my handcuffs and the chain from my neck. Having drawn one to the best of my abilities, they wanted to know what the pommel of the saddle was, for they did not believe my assertions, but put their own constructions on it, Mr. Quan telling me I was a liar. After continuing these sort of questions for some time, they brought in a packet of papers very carefully packed up, which on opening proved to be a file of business letters from Mr. M—— to me, all relating to mercantile affairs, and all about from two and a half to three years old; they related to trade in long-cloths and other merchandize; these must have been taken out of my desk as they were with all the old letters I kept there the fellows seemed to think they had a great prize in them; and I was made to explain them, which I did as I thought proper, as they all related to a vessel which I commanded, prior to taking charge of the brig Ann; the explanations must have been of great use to the Chinese government. The shroff wrote down all I chose to tell him from the letters, and after having finished two or three, Mr. Partridge was brought, and I took the opportunity of telling him what I had said, and cautioning him to be very careful; I was enabled to do this as the mandarins were now at tiffin. After they had done I was sent away, and he had to explain the contents of the same letters over again; there were one or two of my own private letters crossed, and these I told him to say were written in French, and that he could not understand them; at last, about seven o'clock, we were taken to a small hall and had a capital dinner, and abundance of it; having finished, I asked them to let us take away what was left, and after a deal of demur and humbug our request was complied with. I sent by Mr.

Partridge, about half that was left for Gully and his party, taking the rest to my place, where we arrived about 8 p.m., and our half-starved companions very soon discovered what we had taken with us. This mandarin we found out was called the Toti-Tygin, and behaved better to us than any other on the island.

26th.—To-day Mr. Roope and self were had up to Quan's, when we had to explain the remainder of the file of my old letters; I did so as far I deemed prudent, all my explanations being written down in Chinese, I was told they were all to be sent to Foo Chow Foo, and they would then be compared with the translations by some Chinese who understood English, and could read and write that language; this I looked upon only as a lie, and supposed it done to intimidate us, particularly as we were threatened with torture if found to explain them wrong. After having got through several, a bundle was brought in, and on being opened, we saw a military officer's shell jacket, a corporal's coat, and an epaulette, both coat and jacket had green facings and one or two buttons, showing that their owners belonged to the 55th regiment; an examination now commenced about the British army, how organized, &c., what the epaulette was for; they thought it was worn on the head, and asked many, of to us, the most foolish and ridiculous questions imaginable. The articles above alluded to were taken out of the wreck of the transport Nerbudda in September or October last, about which time she was wrecked on this island. Mr. Partridge and the gunner were brought to our prison to-day, from whom we heard that poor Gully was still unwell. I am very anxious to see him. During our absence to-day from the prison, our fellow-captives, we were told, had been kicking up a row among themselves, having, by begging, got cash enough to purchase sufficient quantity of samshu to make them drunk enough to be quarrelsome. Edward Wilson was taken sick to-day.

27th.—I this morning wrote a letter ready to give the carpenter, when an opportunity offers, in the hope he would be able to get it across to Amoy. The weather to day was very rainy with hard squalls. In the afternoon I was sent for by Quan, and on getting to the court-house was surprised at seeing a strange lascar; I could not however speak to him as I was sent back immediately, and Mr. Partridge and the gunner were then taken to the court-house, the latter was, however, directly sent back, and Mr. Partridge detained for the purpose of explaining the rest of the letters to the carpenter who explained them to the shroff and by him they were written in Chinese. Mr. Partridge returned in the evening and told us he said what he thought most prudent about the letters; he had been able to speak to the lascar, who told him he belonged to the Nerbudda, and complained bitterly of the conduct of the captain and officers of that ship, as well as of the way they were treated by the Chinese, being, like ourselves, half or more than half starved. There were, he said, as far as he knew, about 120 men in this town, lascars and camp-followers. He was quite surprised when he heard that the captain, and other Europeans who had left the ship, after she was wrecked, in the long boat, had arrived safe at Macao some months ago.

28th.—Mr. Partridge sent for and employed as yesterday. The mandarins would not let him return, at which I kicked up a bit of a row, not knowing their reasons for keeping him from us all night; some of the clerks, however, soon brought him, when he told us he had seen another lascar belonging to the Nerbudda, who corroborated the former man's statement. The mandarin, it appeared, did not like Mr. Partridge to be with us till the letters were all finished, and as they seldom got more than three done in one day, in consequence of the difficulty of making them understand what he meant, it will take some time as there are about 20 or 30. The fellow thought I told Mr. Partridge what to say, and said I was a bad man and a liar. Mr. Partridge said he had had a good mess of cakes and sweetmeats, also some China wine. In a little time they brought us some, and one of the principal clerks promised he would take care Mr. Partridge had a good bed to sleep on and enough to eat, and pledged his word he should come to no harm. I made no more resistance, which would indeed have been folly in our helpless situation; however, through Mr. Partridge I got the note given to the carpenter I had last written.

May 5th.—Fine morning. I awoke very hungry, but still refused to eat. Quan out all the morning, also our old jailer. The deputy-jailer and guards got frightened on my telling them that I intended to starve myself to death. As I expected to see the carpenter soon, I wrote another letter for Amoy, trusting to chance for an opportunity of getting it sent in the afternoon. Shortly after Quan returned he sent for me and asked what was the reason I did not eat, and what I wanted. I told him I could not live on rice. He asked me what English people lived on; I told him bread, vegetables, and meat. He was greatly surprised on hearing that the staple food in England was not rice, and still more so on being told it was not cultivated there, looking on the English as really a set of barbarians for this very reason. In reply to his questions of what I wanted, I told him that I wanted proper food for all my men and enough of it; also leave to visit them daily, a proper place for all to live in, and for Mr. Gully, Roope, Partridge, and myself to have a separate place from the rest; that we had done them no wrong and were not thieves to be shackled and chained as we were. He said all my complaints should be made known to the head mandarin, but that he had not power of himself to grant my requests, but would do what he could for me. (Oh, these promises, how often have we been deceived by them.) He ordered me some dinner, which I ate and said, " I should have bread instead of rice, also a little China wine and more animal food for the people." While at dinner, I had an opportunity of speaking to the carpenter, who had been sent for as interpreter ; he had not been able to get the last chit I gave him away, but I gave him the one I had written, telling him to send both, if possible, as soon as he could. He said, he had been told, ships were off the place at anchor, and that their boats were out sounding ; that all the principal merchants had left the town, shutting up their shops and taking their valuables with them; and that troops were coming to this town from all parts of the island to strengthen and garrison the town, expecting an attack here from the English; he said, most of the mandarins were in a terrible fright. All these reports he heard from his jailer, who, he said, behaved very well to him, stipulating in return for kindnesses a promise of protection when the place should be taken. On going back to prison, the joy this news gave us cannot be described, nor can it I think be imagined by those who have not been in a similar wretched situation. We shook hands with each other, and it was all we could do to keep from shedding tears; we now had some hopes of deliverance, and thought for the first time of attempting an escape.

9th.—Weather as yesterday: a very strict guard over our prison. Employed all day drawing and painting. In the evening I was taken before Mr. Quan, and questioned about the British men-of-war, their different sizes, and the number of guns they could carry, where the heaviest guns were placed, and many similar questions; he then commenced asking about the capabilities of steamers, their draft of water, &c., and when I told him many were made of iron, he as usual told me I was a liar: however I got the carpenter to ask him leave for me to see my men, and begged he would give them all clothing, of which I knew they were in want; many of them being, as I learnt from the Chinese, in a state of nudity. I also asked for a barber, and said I should like to see the head mandarin again: to all my requests he gave, Chinese-like, any quantity of promises, and again resumed his questions by asking who Smith at Amoy was? Supposing he meant Captain Smith of H.M.S. Druid, I told him he was a man of great power and rank, and was a great English mandarin; and that as soon as he heard the authorities in Formosa had detained Englishmen who had been wrecked on their island as prisoners, he would come over and play the devil with them. He asked many more questions, as was generally the case; they were too numerous and absurd to commit to paper; in fact I could not remember all. After this I was dismissed, but not before I had learnt from the carpenter that he had got my last letters sent to Tamsin (near the place where we were wrecked), where he heard English ships were: the man whom he got to take them promised that if the ships were gone he would forward them to Amoy. The English appear to have many friends here: most of the Chinese I have seen and been able to communicate with, show the greatest disgust and indignation against their own government. I had a very slight repast, not fit to be called a meal, after which I was sent back to prison. No one, I heard, had been allowed to go near them.

11th.—Weather the same as yesterday. Employed as usual drawing. During the day many soldiers came to this establishment; these men were allowed free access to us, and from them we learnt that a number of Chinese had been beheaded. This day they made a great noise, and wished for our pictures, which we gave them; in return we got a small supply of sweet potatoes, which we got the jailer's boy to cook for our supper, and a great treat they were: I thought them delicious, though I formerly could not bear them. Starvation does wonders.

13th. Morning cloudy but day fine. Quan out at daylight. Was told the troops were exercising great guns, which I suppose was true, as we heard many of the reports here. Employed drawing steamers, &c., on fans, for the mandarins' followers. I am getting rather tired of such pastime, and feel the want of books very much. In the afternoon I was taken up before Quan, who wanted to know about the different sizes of men-of-war; the complement of men for each class; quantity and weight of guns, small-arms, shot, &c., and draft of water. The same questions with regard to steamers, when I told him that we likewise had iron steam-boats of a very light draft, he would not believe me, and on telling him that men-of-war were not manned with lascars he told me, as usual, I was a liar.

The carpenter tells me that twenty-two Chinese were beheaded for rebellion the day before yesterday; so there appears to be some truth in what the soldiers told us. He is still very closely confined, and not allowed to speak to any but his jailers, from some of whom he heard that the English had taken some island near here a few days ago, but I could not understand him properly, and know of no islands but the Pescadores near here. When I had answered Quan's questions, I was sent back directly, and got this news from the carpenter on my way back to prison, where I found on my return some of my companions had got a small supply of sweet potatoes, off which we made a tolerable supper.

14th.—Fine weather. We this day got some Chinese soap. It looks like coarse black sand or oatmeal, but of a dark brown or black colour. It was miserable stuff; but with a deal of scrubbing took the dirt off our skins, leaving many scratches.

15th.—Fine weather. More people allowed to visit us, all bringing fans for us to paint on for them, and all wishing the painting to be a steamer.

16th.—In the evening in consequence of the soldiers not allowing us to keep near the outer door of our prison for the purpose of breathing a little fresh air, had a row with them, which speedily brought the head-jailer and all his gang, about ten or twelve. Thinking this was a good opportunity for getting more space allowed us to live in, I determined to try for it, and commenced by giving the soldier, when he returned from calling the gang, a bit of a licking, and then taking old Quat (the head-jailer of the establishment) and his right-hand man by the throats, I swore I would knock their heads together till they were half dead if we were not allowed more space to live in, as we could not, confined as we were, breathe. I asked him how he expected we could live in such a hole, so closely confined this hot weather. After a deal of pros and cons we were allowed to sleep in the outer jailer's room, and for my use they sent for, and speedily brought, a bamboo trestle bed-place and a mat;

they also brought us about a dozen pieces of pine-apple and sugar-cane, about the size of the top of my thumb, at the same time begging us to make no noise. After this I made them promise to take down the large mats in front of the windows to-morrow, in order that if there is any wind we may get a little of it. This promise was not performed.

20th.—In the afternoon I saw two of our lascars in the front yard in chains. They were not allowed to come near us, but the soldiers say they have refused to eat their food, it being very bad, and cooked or mixed up with pork fat.

22d.—Continued fine weather. During the day I was taken up before Quan, who repeated the questions he asked yesterday, and received the same answers, all as near the truth as I knew. I was afterwards taken out with the carpenter and shroff to an inner yard, where we had to wait till the evening, when Quan came out followed by a number of clerks, their friends, and about ten soldiers. They brought out a long table with a large roll of English paper, which on opening I saw was a chart of the English channel; this he wanted explained, asking question after question, to all of which I gave him answers as correct as I could. When London was pointed out to him he seemed very pleased; asked the size of it; where the queen lived; how many houses and inhabitants it contained; how far it was; and how long it took an English ship to go from Canton to London; whether any Chinese junks went there: but it is quite impossible to recollect all he asked. He went from the French to the English coast and back again, asking the names of every mark or line on the chart. As it now began to get dark he said he should send for me to-morrow. I thought this a good opportunity again to speak about new quarters; but like every thing on this island, except for their own gratification, he said he would tell me to-morrow. I also told him that before our old jailer left us, he had borrowed from me two mace and 35 cash (this was part of the money given Mr. Roope and me by the mandarins as formerly mentioned), and had forgot to pay it; he said he would get it back for me. It was to-day the carpenter told me of the shroff receiving two mace per day from the mandarins, as mentioned some time ago, all of which he appropriated to his own use, refusing his shipmates who are with him a single cash. Returned back to jail as usual, but in better health, having no fever.

23d.—Fine weather, but very hot. Taken up to the mandarin, and the chart brought out; the names of most of the large places on the coasts of England, France, &c., written in Chinese and stuck on the chart. The mandarin thinks it is a very great prize, and wants to know how far it is. I suppose he will propose making a fleet of ships and steamers, and to take it. I told him about steam coaches, at which he seemed much surprised, and wants a train drawn.

I told him if he would let Mr. Gully come here and help me, I would draw him one. He promised to do so to-morrow, as it is the only chance of our meeting that I can see at present. Had dinner in the yard, and was afterwards taken back to our horrid place of confinement. While up, asked the mandarin to let us have a barber; he said he would speak to the head mandarin about it. My face a little better, but still very painful.

26th.—Employed drawing and painting. Very dull and monotonous. Wrote a letter to Mr. Gully. Quang took it and promised to deliver it. Very anxious to see Gully. This evening I took a good spell at Aquat's opium pipe, to make me sleep. It made me feel very ill and sick, but I went to sleep almost immediately.

27th.—Fine day, with fresh S.W. wind. Very ill, and vomited several times during the day. I can eat nothing of any kind. It is the last time I will touch opium. About 2 p. m., was greatly pleased to see Gully brought here. I was sent for and found him employed drawing a railway train, &c. Had a long yarn with him, and dinner was brought to us in the yard. This made me sick again, the sight of the food being enough to turn my stomach; I was unable to touch any thing.

31st.—Fine weather. Employed as yesterday. On returning in the evening to prison, a letter from Forbes was put into my hand, in answer to one of mine of the 10th of April. His is dated the 14th instant. Of course we are all highly pleased that our friends know where we are. The man who brought it promising to come to-morrow for an answer, as he could not stop. I am very sorry I did not see him. Wrote an answer and enclosed the letter. I gave it to Quang Leon, ready for the man should he come for it during my absence to-morrow. Thank God, there is some chance now of our leaving this horrid place. Mr. Gully and Newman still unwell.

June 3d.—Very little for dinner. On sending for more it was refused, in return for which I broke all the basins and plates, and smashed the rice kid. Quat highly delighted at the fun; the jailers will not come near us; I suppose they are afraid of being pounded. In the evening, about eight o'clock, they sent us about forty bread cakes, and Quang Leon brought us some China wine, to make up for short allowance. Their excuse being that we could have no more grub because it rained; consequently, if it rains for a week, I suppose we are to starve. During one of the squalls, about midnight, we felt a severe shock of an earthquake, which lasted about two minutes. The floor and walls of our prison shook so violently as to wake all but two of us.

4th.—Dark, squally, cloudy weather, with hard rain at times. No postman returned as yet. I suppose he is off to his own town, which is some distance from this. Mr. Gully is better. In the afternoon the long and anxiously wished for postman came.

Gave him a letter to Captain Forbes. He could not stop, and appeared timid. He gave me about one mace in cash and a small pot of China wine, for which he got a picture, to make it appear that he came to buy one; and started off directly. This evening I got some more rhubarb from Quang Leon for Gully.

5th.—Flying showers of rain. Stinking salt-fish for breakfast, which I refused to eat; and up to this time, 2 p.m. have sent about a dozen times for the head jailer, but without success. I am keeping some as a specimen to show to the mandarin what sort of fare we get. Finding that no one came, I walked up to the court, much to the surprise of every clerk and soldier present, and then waited with what I had kept from breakfast. Quat in a fright ran for Gully and Roope. At last we saw the mandarin, who took the cook's part, but promised us better food and more of it, and ordered us some dinner. The shroff and carpenter were brought up to interpret. We were shortly after taken before the mandarin again, to see poor Quat get a licking. It appears that it was requisite that some one should be punished to appease the mandarin's indignant feelings, so poor Quat was picked out. We were told, that if the emperor knew we went out of prison without a guard, or permission, he would be very angry; and that the mandarin had flogged Quat to let us see what he would do to us, if the offence was repeated. We told him he had better try it, after which he went out and had some chow chow. One of the head clerks told me that the boy was flogged for stealing our food, though they knew that he could not do so, and that the cooks stole it. As I had been told more than once that they did so, I promised the pair of them a thorough good licking when they came with the evening grub. They got to the windward of me, however, by sending two strange men with the dinner, which was very good. At night, Quat got as drunk as a lord, and told us what he would do to the mandarin when the English came, which by the by, all classes appear very anxious for, but the mandarins.

9th.—A cloudy day. Some kind of religious chin chinning going on outside. Quat's assistant gets a licking from Mr. Roope, for not cooking some potatoes for him, and allowing the soldier to steal half of them. Medicine does its duty, take congou and feel a deal better. All very still up to this time, 3 p.m. Observe that most of the Chinese had a piece of yellow paper on the end of their tails. About 5 p.m., some of the head clerks came for Mr. Gully; he was ironed and sent away. They said the big mandarin wanted him, but I think it all a lie to get him back to his other prison. They tell us he is to come back in four or five days.

10th.—A very fine day. I get hold of a pair of

scissors, and cut my beard off as close as I can : the boy in a fright about it; he says he shall be flogged if the mandarin knows of it. Quat is visited by two of his countrymen. Many large trays containing hams, fruit, fowls, ducks, sweetmeats, &c., carried about all day from joss-house to joss-house. In the evening we had a scene from Mr. Wilson and Mr. Roope about cards, which ended in the cards being put into the bucket.

11th.—Continued fine weather. Chin-chinning going on as yesterday. I received a letter from Mr. Gully, who tells me he is in his old prison.

18th.—Tee-sy-yea gave us a fine piece of fish, and at dinner the mandarin sent us a fowl. All things considered, we spent this day as well as could be expected, and drank the health of the Duke of Wellington. I can't think why the mandarin was so liberal, perhaps he has heard how they will be treated if we are ill used. [In consequence of messes of putrid greens and rice, salt-fish and fat pork being served from day to day to the prisoners for dinner, Captain Denham became very ill. On the 28th he began to recover. His complaints were never attended to, though promises of amendment were incessantly made, but made apparently with no object but to put off the complaint for the time, there not being any real intention to redress it.]

July 2d.—Another fine morning. I receive a

note from Wilson, who tells me the shroff has been up alone before the mandarin this morning, that for the last three days a great quantity of hand and leg irons (new) have arrived. There have also been brought here nine cages which are placed in the yard before their prisons. Some people have told them we are going away. The nine cages correspond with our numbers in that respect. As far as regards Mr. Roope and self, and our late fellow prisoners, that there is more going on than we are aware of is very likely. I answer their note and tell them not to leave until we all meet, and I write the same to the lascars. The day very still.

3rd.—Still finer weather. Employed drawing, &c. In the afternoon got Chu Sam y ats to bring the carpenter and shroff up, and asking the latter for what purpose he had been before the mandarin; he said it was about two Canton men, to see if he could recognise them. This I think only an excuse of his. The carpenter tells me he is in league with the mandarins, and has promised them that he will say what they wish. There are many men hired by the mandarins to say that the vessel was taken in action. Some men are in prison for refusing to say so, and I also hear that between twenty and thirty men were drowned in plundering the wreck. The mandarins received a letter a few days ago from the other side, and are all promoted for *taking* the brig, they having reported that, on seeing her they sent their men-of-war out, shot away her masts, killing most of her men, drove the vessel on shore, and took what men remained prisoners. To this the carpenter tells me the shroff has said yes, and is a great favourite with the mandarins. I think the rascal is bargaining for his own life by selling us. We got Chu Sam y ats to let us have one mace a day each, instead of being fed from the Chinese cook-house. This, I hope, will enable us to live without so much rice and slush, pork fat, &c.

4th.—A fine day. Before breakfast we were ironed and taken, with the carpenter and shroff, before the bluebuttons. I was the only one taken to see them. The questions asked were chiefly about England, the size of London, where the queen lived, and if they could get to London by water; if Sir H. Pottinger was a white or black man, his age, size, &c.; also if the English could walk to America in a week, and if the English had ever fought with the Dutch. I told them yes; and on being asked what for, I replied it was for putting Englishmen in prison and plundering them. They then asked how many countries the English had got. I told all I could recollect, and added Hong Kong, Amoy, Chusan, Chinghai, Ningpoo, and Hauchowfoo; this the carpenter said he could not tell them as he would be flogged if he did. Among other questions they wanted to know what English mandarin died after taking Canton. I told them Sir F. Senhouse. They were also very anxious to know what sort of a mandarin Capt. Smith was, at Amoy. I told him a No. 1 mandarin, and most likely they would see him soon. This the carpenter also refused to tell them. There was a strange mandarin there, with a transparent crystal button.

8th.—Wind and weather as yesterday. About 3 p.m. clearing up a little, plainly saw the eclipse, the sun being nearly obscured made the afternoon very dark. Many of the mandarin's gang very anxious to know if we have such phenomena in our part of the world, also if it rains the same there as it does on this island.

9th.—Dark cloudy day with heavy rain for the most part of it. Every thing in our prison is cold, damp, and miserable. The very mats we sleep on being covered with mould from the dampness. The evening fine; I feel unwell.

10th.—A very fine day, have a good clean out, and place every moveable out in the sun to dry. Still unwell. Four months to-day since we were wrecked, and two months since they received my letter at Amoy. What can they be doing to let us remain so long; for all I see to the contrary we are likely to be four months more here. We feel the want of books very much. I received a letter from Mr. Gully who has heard that a ship has been lost at Tamseu or Khelau, and all hands drowned.

In the evening the carpenter was brought up to tell us we must not draw any more pictures, as he says, if the head mandarin knows it he will be very angry. It strikes me there is more in this than we are aware of. The carpenter says the mandarin is afraid we shall be sending letters over to Amoy. At night, about half past twelve, I was roused up to go and see Kitchil, and found him very ill and light-headed, but without fever; gave him a dose of rhubarb and covered him well up. Wilson also sick; hear that all the paper and ships, &c. which they had, were taken away, and they were forbidden to draw any more. They were, however, paid for what was taken away.

11th.—A fine day. Before breakfast we were taken away in irons to the head mandarin's, who now has a red button (so that there is some truth in the report about their being promoted, as he before wore a blue one); but prior to going, Ayum came to us, requesting if we were asked, that we would say we had only drawn two ships; for, if the big man knew we had drawn more, our lotier would get into a scrape. On arriving there, we saw the chap (he is governor of this island), and another one with a white transparent button, these being the only two mandarins. There Mr. Partridge and the gunner were also taken, but no Mr. Gully. His first question was, if I had breakfasted, and then commenced about geography, till at last

I had to draw him a map of the world, as well as I could. He was very anxious to know what islands and colonies belonged to Great Britain, and had them all marked. He had a book which they both frequently referred to, asking many questions about the distances of different places from each other. About three p. m. we were taken out to a capital breakfast, which we all did justice to. (I forgot to mention that three lascars and four Portuguese sea-cunnies were also brought here to-day, I suppose for him to see, as he asked no questions of them.) After our repast we again set to work about the map, and at between five and six we knocked it off. He then asked many questions about the Queen and Prince Albert, wishing to know if her Majesty had more than one husband, and many, to us, absurd questions. He appeared to think it very strange that a country should be governed by a woman. He gave Mr. Roope, Mr. Partridge, the gunner, and self, five mace each, and the lascars and sea-cunnies three mace each. We then requested to be allowed to see Mr. Gully, and also asked him to let us five live together at his place. The former request he granted, and said we should see Mr. Gully to-morrow; and said he would get a place made for us to live in, at present having none large enough or ready, and he took down our names. After leaving, I was twice called back; once he asked, in an apparently careless manner if I had written to Amoy. I should have told him yes, and received an answer; but the carpenter begged me not, and, fearing that I should get some of those who were kind to us at our place into trouble, I said "No." The other time was to tell me, when I left this, not to trade in opium again, as it was very bad. Among some of the questions about Sir H. Pottinger, the shroff very politely told the mandarin I was a liar. But on the whole, I am pleased with this interview. It strikes me that the authorities here have received some letters from over the water, telling them to mind what they are about with us. I can account for this change in no other way. Jumaul, lascar, says that we are the third vessel wrecked on this island, and that there are, besides the Nerbudda's people and us another ship's company prisoners. I can hardly credit this; had it been the case I think we should have heard of it, as they were wrecked prior to the Nerbudda; he did not know the name of the vessel. I hear that lately all our lascars have had jackets and trousers given them, and also beside their food they are allowed four cash a day each. I feel certain in my own mind there is something at the back of all this. [The examination of the 11th was renewed on the following day, and the oft-repeated questions about the queen again asked, and the answers doubted, because, though perfectly true, they were unintelligible to the Chinese.]

21st.—Moderate breeze and cloudy weather; very hot. Before breakfast a party of our lascars came to our prison to tell us Jamsu had just died. Medicine had not been sent him, but some was now brought by the head jailer and given me for him. (The jailer knew the man was dead, and I believe only brought it to say that medicine had been given for him.) The lascars' prison is very damp, close, and unhealthy, and they persist in saying Satan has got among them; that they will all die unless removed. I promise to do my best for them, requesting them all to remain quiet for two or three days. I get an interview with the mandarin, find our carpenter and shroff acting there as interpreters for the Nerbudda's crew, whose names, ages, &c. are being taken down. I tell the mandarin that the place the people are in is not fit to live in; that two men have died during the week, and insist upon a more suitable one for all of us; that the sick are not properly attended to, and end by requesting an interview with the redbutton. He says of himself he can do nothing without orders, but will speak to the head mandarin and let me know the result. I got him to promise he would send a letter to the redbutton for me; this, after some demur, he said he would. I return to the lascars and tell them the result. They promise to remain quiet for some three days longer, and if no notice is then taken they will all come out and refuse to return to their present place of confinement any more. They go back so far satisfied. The mandarin would not allow me to see the corpse buried. Jamsu had only been ill a week, and the night before he died he vomited two live worms, about eight inches long. I this morning saw some of the Nerbudda's people. Many of them appear fine healthy men, but some are sad objects, having lost the use of their limbs. The carpenter tells me he has seen the names of 144 men, how many more there are he does not know. I write an official letter to the governor of the island, in which I explain our wants and complain of the inattention paid to the sick here, the damp unhealthy places of confinement we are all in, and request a speedy interview. Having no seal, I paste the letter in an envelope and paint a flagstaff with the union jack over the join. This from the circumstance of our mandarin giving a party to-day, I am unable to give him and refuse to deliver it into any one's hands but his own. There is a theatre rigged in the mandarin's court-house, and all the knights of sock and buskin are performing in fine style to the sound of gongs and other such like discordant sounds. In the evening get a glimpse of the performance. Dresses very rich, much pantomime, and no shift of scene, but one or two seem to perform very well. The part of females acted by men, and so well disguised that I should be deceived at first sight. The mandarins' wives and concubines were invisible to vulgar eyes, being placed behind a screen, from which they could see and hear all that was going on, without fear of being seen.

22d.—Beautiful weather but very hot. Early in the morning was called by Kitchil to go and see Wilson, who had been ill during the night. I went and did all in my power for him by placing towels dipped in hot water on his stomach. I took the same opportunity of visiting the lascars. All well but one. They complain dreadfully of the heat, and the place is really unfit for a dog to live in, they having to sleep on the stone flooring, through which the wet rises during the night and makes them cold and stiff. This, with the extreme heat during the day, causes such an effluvia to arise as would put any one into a fever. I write about this to the mandarin, go straight to the court-house and give the letter to Chu Sam y ats, telling him at the same time I want a speedy answer. He promises to deliver it, and I return to my den. I afterwards hear he is off to some distant place to officiate at an execution.

26th.—Fine wind and weather. In the morning our mandarin goes out, I hear about some murder, and am told he will not return for three or four days. Wilson not so well to-day: self the same. To-day see part of a marriage ceremony; the bride being carried about on a platform with artificial flowers, &c. On the platform was also a young kid, chained by the neck to a rose-tree, at her feet. The bridesmaid (as I suppose she was) was on another similar vehicle, with a quantity of imitation jewels, &c. In the evening I saw the latter again standing on the back of a flying stork, made of paper and bamboo: she was singing, or rather screaming, and accompanied her melody by playing on a kind of guitar: an old man was playing a reed similar in sound to a boy's penny trumpet. Mr. Gully's mandarin officiates here to-day. I write a letter to Gully, and get the pipebearer to take it for me. Two culprits condemned to lose their left hand, the impression of which was taken on paper, and sent to the governor for his sanction.

28th and 29th.—Squally rainy weather. Feel worse instead of better. Go to Chu Sam y ats', who sends for a doctor and the carpenter: he prescribes, and I get dosed with medicines. The doctor says my illness is caused either by drinking cold water, taking rhubarb, or eating a pig's bladder. The water he knows is bad, and rhubarb they appear to think a most dangerous medicine, next to poison. Old Chu Sam y ats gets a jar, and now gives us good water. Our mandarin returns. Our place yet damp and miserable. I trust we are not to remain in this infernal island another five months: the doctor tells me that plenty of people die at this time of the year. Very pleasant reflection to die rotting in a jail, within a few miles of an English force sufficient to take the whole island.

10th.—A fine day. Five months since we were

cast away, and three months since they received my letter at Amoy. Before breakfast Mr. Partridge and the gunner came, and we were told we were all to go to the Redbutton's. They also brought the serang and first tindal of the Nerbudda: they had not met before for nine months: also one of our lascars (Jumaul). We all had our handcuffs, and were taken away in chairs with a larger guard than usual. On going outside the gates it struck me we were going to our promised new house. After going about three-quarters of a mile, we came to a large mandarin's house where we got out. A great many soldiers were about, many of whom had arms. We were taken into a sort of yard, where we saw the carpenter, shroff, and Isidore, sea-cunnies. The carpenter told me this was a "No. 1 large soldier mandarin," and that we must chin chin him. This I promised to do. After a time our lotier and Mr. Gully's arrived; also our fellow's deputy, and many others, most of whom were, I believe, military. The carpenter and shroff were then taken away, and shortly returned, telling me I must knock head three times. I told him I would not, thinking it was the wish of the understrappers, &c. He again went away, and shortly after returned bringing some of our lotier's followers with him, and begged me to do so, as it would cause a deal of cow cow if I did not. I told him I would of course salute the mandarin, but not cow tow unless obliged. He then went away, and shortly afterwards I was called on to appear before this great man. I walked on, and on turning the court facing him, I must say I was surprised at the display. There were about twenty-five Chinese officers in full dress (a very handsome one), on each side forming a kind of lane. They had their swords by their sides. At the upper end of these two lines was a raised place, about ten inches above the ground on which they stood, and here on my left were three high mandarins, one red and two bluebuttons, each with arms and a peacock's feather in his cap. They were standing, as were all except the head mandarin. On the right stood a gang of interpreters and a few common soldiers in the back. In front of us was the man himself seated behind a table, on which were writing materials, &c.; and round him were fifteen or eighteen mandarins of all ranks, if I may judge from their dresses and buttons in their caps. On reaching the raised place on which the carpenter and shroff were, I saluted the mandarin, and sat on the ground. At this he shouted out most lustily, and I was forced to go on my knees. The carpenter then said I must knock head. I refused, and drawn swords were round me in a twinkling. Finding I must do as they wish I do so with a very bad grace, my blood boiling, and looking as red, I believe, as the button on the mandarin's cap before me. He then went on talking to those around him, and appeared in an awful rage. The carpenter was terribly frightened, and I was kept on my knees. His first question, after about half a dozen reasons why I should be obliged to cow tow, was, who was the head man on board a ship. I said the captain, and told the carpenter I should sit down, as remaining in that position hurt me. He begged me not. I then requested him to ask leave for me to sit. He says he did ask, but I saw no notice taken of it, and no answer was given. He then sent for the rest of the party; and as they came, I told them they must knock head, it was useless resisting. They all did so, but he saw it was with a very ill will, and kept us on our knees. They were behind me on the lower place, the mandarin raised a step above. He then asked how many ships there were at Canton, Amoy, and to the northward. I told the carpenter I did not know, and could answer no questions in that position. I am mistaken: his first question was, had I written to Amoy. I replied no. He then asked who had, but I said I was not aware. He said if we had not written, how could they have heard about us being here, and have received letters about it. I again said I did not know, and supposed the junkmen had told them. On my refusing to answer questions, he waited a little; I suppose he did not know I said so, as I think the people would frame some excuse for fear of being punished, if they said such a thing. They then brought in a sheep, and he asked what it was, and what ship it came from, also what it was for. The tindal told him it was from the Nerbudda, and was to eat; that there were three on board when lost. They then took it away and brought in a dog. He asked what that was for, if it was for eating. The tindal told him it was for catching rats, and a sort of pet, &c. The poor beast appeared much frightened and very ill, apparently half starved. It was then taken away. At this time I was in great pain from the position in which I was obliged to remain. All my weight on my knees, on a brick floor: the perspiration was pouring down me. I attempted to sit on my legs, but was roused up immediately. The mandarin then wanted to know why we appeared before him without leg-irons. And orders were given, and a bag full of very stout leg-irons and new locks was brought in, and also some chains. Our legs were then put in irons, and new locks put on our handcuffs; this, with the chain necklaces, completed our ornaments. We were then again placed on our knees. After a short time he sent us away to breakfast; and went also himself. This appears to be a very extensive establishment, repairs were going on, in the place we were taken breakfast and gun-carriages were being made. On our way to this part of the place, we passed two of the brig's guns (six-pounders), they were mounted on new carriages. They have a large quantity of all kinds of arms here in capital order, and very clean. They are placed in racks. There are also several carriage-guns (about twelve or fifteen), the largest I should say, about four pounds. Our breakfast (which was a capital one, and enough for the whole ship's company had they been there) we would not touch. One of the bluebutton mandarins had to superintend, but all the coaxing, &c. would not do. The carpenter and shroff were the only two who ate any thing. In about an hour we were again called for, and I promised the chaps that I would cow tow this time. (Pride shall have a fall.) We were taken into a small room and made our obeisance, Chinese fashion. He then sent all out but Mr. Partridge, the two Chinamen, and myself. His guards were all unarmed, but standing near him. He then, on our asking him, allowed us to sit down. He wished to know the number of decks, and guns in an English ship of large size, and the weight of the guns, on which deck the heaviest were placed, &c. A box was then brought in and opened, out of which was taken the Ann's coloured glass signal lamp. I explained the use of it. The other things brought out were a military officer's coat with green facings but no buttons, an officer's epaulette, a tell-tale compass (no card), my sextant, a quadrant, a small lascar's looking-glass, a masonic apron, the Nerbudda's rudder chains, and a pair of bobstays. The use of all these was made known to him. He then asked me if I had any spy-glasses on board. I told him four. He asked what was the value of one, and I informed him that the prices varied according to the article, from 10 dollars to 100 dollars. The next question was, how many glasses were inside one, and how far we could see with a good one. He then wanted to know if I could mend my sextant. I told him no; it must go to England to be repaired. He inquired whether I could get another in Canton. Answer yes, for 150 dollars. How far could an Englishman walk in a day. I replied thirty miles. He did not keep us very long, and told us, on going away, that if the mandarins wished to put irons on us we must allow it, as it was the custom of the country, and that the next time we came we must cow tow, as that was custom. He took our hand-irons off during the examination. We were then taken away. On being told we had eaten no breakfast, one of the bluebuttons came up to me and told me not to be afraid; that they would not cut our heads off. The redbutton, I believe, told him to say so, as he laughed and thought we did not eat, because we were afraid. I am sorry for this, as I wished him to have a very different opinion, and told him I did not eat because I was not well, not because I was frightened. He only laughed, and appeared to disbelieve me. He is a very fine-looking man, I should say 38 or 40 years old, and wears an opaque red button and peacock's feather with two eyes in it. This I believe is a very high rank, the emperor having only three in his. We were taken out by a different way from the one we entered by, and placed in our chairs again, with a strong guard. We were not taken to our former prison. On our way we passed a guard-house, and saw a great many armed soldiers. I now began to think they intended to take us to some other town more inland, but my fears on this account were soon at rest, for we shortly stopped, I should say not half a mile from the mandarin's house. We were then taken out and led into a small joss-house, joining our present place of confinement, when we saw Chu Sam y ats, who with our servant Low had brought our bed places and mats, &c. I asked for Mr. Gully to be brought, and our mandarin, who followed us, said he would ask the big man to-morrow. I told him I would rather be as before unless Mr. Gully was allowed to be with us; and he promised that if on the morrow the mandarin would not let Mr. Gully come, he would take us back to our old quarters. The lying rascal! I don't believe him. Our prison is a fine large room, about twenty-seven feet by seventeen, and lofty. Next to us, but divided by a thick wall, are our guards, about twenty in number. We have a place outside our room for walking in wet weather, as long as the two rooms are wide, and outside is a yard about ninety feet long by ten or twelve broad. I like the change every way, except as to the absence of Mr. Gully, all chance of communication with him is, I am sorry to say, cut off. Why they have brought one sea-cunny, one lascar, and two of the Nerbudda's people with me, I am at a loss to conceive, but here we are all in the same room. They have given each a bamboo trestle-bed, and mat, a basin, chopsticks, and a plate; there are a water jar, two cooking pots, a teapot, two cups, two stools, two small tables, and these, I believe, with a tin cooking pot, complete the furniture of our house. On asking Chu Sam y ats to take our irons off, he promised he would do so at dinner time. We waited till then, and it was again, after lots of excuses, postponed till bedtime, and at last till to-morrow morning. I told him we would not eat in irons. He left and said he would ask. I gave him ten minutes, but not coming back in that time, I broke my handcuffs, and almost all soon followed my example of taking them off. We had dinner, but two men who could not get their irons off, had to wait till night, when Chu Sam y ats's servant brought a key that would not open them. We then broke both at his request. He said our leg irons would be taken off to-morrow. They are very stout, and I am afraid if not taken off we shall be obliged to keep them on, as their thickness will baffle our strength. I think myself, that the mandarin's reason for sending me here, is to prevent the possibility of my sending letters across; but thank God he is too late. The day the fellow promised to let

Mr. Gully come and see me, the junk man, our old letter-man, went to Mr. Gully's prison and showed him a paper from Forbes, stating that he was the man who had taken my letter. Mr. Gully immediately wrote a letter, which the man called for next day, and took without being seen by any one, saying he was off directly for Amoy; God send him safe over. Thus far, how fortunate the mandarins did not keep their word. Had Mr. Gully been taken to our quarters, this perhaps last and only chance of writing would have been lost. The man, I think, must have lost my last letter, by his bringing no answer; but let us be thankful for this last chance. Oh! how much I wish to see Gully, but fear it is not to be. He will be very lonesome by himself. No one to speak to. I hope the thoughts of an answer will cheer him up a bit. I went to bed, but not to sleep until just daylight.

13th.—A cloudy squally morning. About 8 o'clock a. m., heard a tremendous crash, and ran out to see what it was that caused it. Found the house next ours, in which were our guards, had fallen. One man was buried in the ruins and two hurt slightly. Mr. Roope, the gunner, and myself immediately ran, and with our hands extricated the man, fortunately still living but much cut about the head. He was taken away after we washed him. I really think his comrades would have let him perish, as they made not the slightest effort to dig him out, but stood pointing and howling like a set of frightened cowards (as they are). We were immediately shifted two doors off nearer the entrance of this place, and quartered in a joss-house. Our Lee Lotier soon came and offered us money for saving the man's life. This we rejected, and only asked to have our leg irons taken off. He promised to apply for leave to do so, and appeared much chagrined at our refusing his money. I am in hopes this may lead to our seeing or getting Mr. Gully to live with us. He must be very lonesome with no one to speak to. I sent him a note to-day, but am doubtful if he will ever get it. Our situation (with the exception of the leg irons, and stoppage of communications,) is in every respect better than before. Night clearing up a little.

16th.—Make a bag for the purpose of secreting my journal. On the 10th instant Gully sent me his log for the purpose of taking care of. I think this bad policy; for if I am searched I shall lose his as well as my own. Nothing occurred till the evening, when we managed to get one leg-iron off; thanks to our guard who supplied us with levers and line. A little rain during the night.

18th.—I think we shall all get well again if we stop here long. We only want Gully to be with us. I am very anxious to hear from or see him. Write him to-day in hopes a chance of sending a letter may soon occur. Query.—Can we be better treated by order of the mandarin, or is it for being the fortunate means of saving the soldier's life? Whatever it may be I am very much pleased at the change.

19th.—Fine weather. Walk about in the yard five miles before breakfast. Add a little to my yarn to Gully. Soldiers tell us that Low Ling has informed the mandarin of our having broken our hand and leg-irons. Nothing occurred.

20th.—Fine weather; cleared out our place, also the yard. Yesterday walked five, and to-day three miles before breakfast. The wounded soldier came to-day to chin chin us, it being the first day he had been out. He is much cut about the face, head, and breast, and is otherwise greatly bruised, but doing well.

22d.—Put in irons and taken to the fort mentioned before, and close to our old quarters.

23d.—A fine day, and fresh breeze, but not for us. No room to walk about. Send for the lee lotier, but cannot get him to bring the carpenter here, so can come to no understanding with him. As usual he is full of promises. Very poor breakfast, and no chance of any improvement. Oh, for books of any kind, what would I now give. After breakfast our guard allowed us to look at what appears to have been the principal entrance to the building. Saw at once that it was the work of Europeans. Most likely the Portuguese. On an inscription over the door, though much defaced and broken, were the following letters and figures:

F. F. E. C. T.

ANNO 1054.

There had originally been much more, but all traces are obliterated; it was some height from us, or we might perhaps have been able to make a little more of it. This proves the men were correct when they told us it was built, if not by the English by other foreigners. We got the door open and went in. It was damp and full of dirt and vermin, and a quantity of bats, which made a most discordant noise. The place, as far as we could get, is full of archways and small cells, all with arched roofs, some larger than others. The stink inside was very bad, and glad I was to get out again; we could go no further in than we did. Seeing no more passages, I suppose they are all blocked up with dirt. It is all in ruins, and appears to have been a kind of monastery. I should say the part we inhabit was originally meant for a chapel. Though, God knows tis not much like one now. We are in a kind of shed more than a house, and I expect the first shower will wash us all out. No chance of getting a letter to Gully, but write one ready.

26th.—Fine weather. We break down one of the small inner doors of our rooms, and burn part of it, in the hope of getting some of the mandarins' people to us. As yet without success. The burra-tindal of the Nerbudda told me to-day, that two months ago, when in prison on the east side of this building (where I believe a large part of her crew now are), a hanger-on about their prison told him there were five English ships off the place. He bribed him with some money to let him go on the walls. He agreed, and on getting up, he declares he saw three European ships off the town. The man told him the other two could not be seen from where he stood, but that there were five ships in all. They had no ensigns hoisted, from which I conclude they were not men-of-war. Their sails were furled. I can only suppose it was some of our friends from Chimoo and Amoy, vainly trying for our liberation by ransom. I think it likely they were told we had been sent away, as was the case, I believe, with the Nerbudda's people. Hear to-day from a Padu who resides close to us, that we are to be sent away in a junk in eight days, but he will not tell us to what place. Continued short allowance. The breaking and burning the door has the desired effect, as this evening one of the men from the mandarin's gang came and spoke about the grub. He offered us three mace a day, but this not being enough, we declined it; when he said he would give us five mace a day, find us in water, and give us a little cooked rice. To this we agreed. We lashed two beds together, when a party got on the top of our prison, and from thence to the walls of this building; the tindal taking a note, in the hopes that from his former prison they might be able to send it to our men; but on reaching the wall over it, he found all the men had been removed, but where or when was impossible for us to find out. Thus is our only chance of communicating with our unfortunate fellow-sufferers cut off. There may be some truth in the yarn about our going away. God only knows when or how our imprisonment will end—every thing is left to conjecture. "Hope deferred truly maketh the heart sick."

27th.—Fine weather. Hear this morning that all the prisoners, with the exception of us eight, have been removed to another town. Patience, patience, for truly we want it. Discontinue notes to Gully, being uncertain when I can have a chance of sending them to him. I am short of paper. The report about the others being removed is, I find, true, but I think not out of this town. In the evening go on the top of this building, and have a look round the town, which, with its suburbs, appears very large and thickly populated. There are many junks at anchor in the bay, which is formed by an extensive reef which joins the fortified island off this town. I think there are several passages in, but we could not make out exactly. There are a small fleet of mandarins' boats and three junks just abreast of us.

29th. — A beautiful morning. Directly after breakfast some soldiers came, and we were all put in irons, hands and feet, and told we were going to the governor's. They said Messrs. Roope and Partridge, with me, were to go first. We were taken out very quietly, but had no chairs, and soon saw we were not going as they had told us. We passed close to our old joss-house, and shortly after came to another larger one, with a paved yard. Here we were halted, and I was taken in first. On reaching what appeared to be the principal entrance, I saw our mandarin, Quan, with a gang of his friends and clerks, and about thirty or forty soldiers, all armed. Time was not given me to make the usual salaam. I was seized by the hair of my head, and hove on the ground. Then Quan ordered the brutes to examine my irons. The handcuffs, I suppose, were considered sufficiently strong, but the leg-irons were hauled off, which hurt me, and scratched and bruised my legs. Another pair was then brought (very thick and heavy, about eight or ten calties): these were put on, and inclosing the legs, they fairly drove them into my flesh. Expostulation was useless. I was spit on and abused: it prevented me putting my right foot to the ground. I was then dragged by the legs and hair to the end of the place, and carried about twenty yards to the back of where this gang of brutes was, and seated on the ground. Messrs. Roope and Partridge were then taken in and served the same way. Mr. Roope was afterwards brought out, but not placed near enough to me to speak. I was then taken back, hove down in the same way, and pulled up on my knees again by the hair of my head. I now saw the carpenter and shroff. The first question Quan asked me was why I went on the roof of our prison, and so on to the fort walls. I told him I did so to have a look round, not knowing I was doing any harm, as the soldier who acted as our guard not only made no objection, but pointed out the place where we could get the best view from. He then asked me why I had broken a plate. This I denied, not having done so; but I have since found out that some days ago one was broken by the gunner. He then spoke about the door being broken; and then asked why we burnt a piece of bamboo. We certainly had burnt this; but it was a short piece, and I should say had been kicking about in the yard for years, as it was quite rotten, and could have been put to no use whatever. He then said the next time I did so he would flog me; and that if a plate was broken, no matter if by accident, he would flog me: he then said he would show me how. I was now seized by seven of the soldiers, and dragged a little further back, still on my knees.

Two of them stood on the calves of my legs, another fixed his knee in my back, one held each shoulder, and two my head by the hair and beard. In this position my trousers were hauled up, and fifty blows given on the front of my thighs with a stick about two and a half inches thick, a kind of Penang lawyer. A fresh man was had for each ten blows. Thanks to pride and pluck I did not sing out: this appeared to make Quan furious: he turned red in the face, stood up and talked on at a furious rate; his eyes glistened as if under strong excitement. After these fifty my right elbow was held out (the arm being bent) in a horizontal position, and the other end of the stick used. There was a knob or head to it. With this I received thirty blows; as before, a fresh man for every ten. One was abused for not striking harder, and the stick given to another wretch. No fault could be found in this respect with this fellow, still I would not cry out, but twice could not help groaning, the pain was so acute. When the thirty were finished, our mandarin's deputy ran up to me and then to the mandarin, chin chinning him not to torture me any more, and after a little bustle I was made to cow tow to Quan. Mr. Partridge was present all the time; he, as well as the carpenter, chin chinned for me, but to no purpose. I was now carried out (the mandarin said he would on the next offence give us short allowance of food) and placed as before on the ground, my legs raw and bleeding, and my elbow in a sad state. I nearly fainted: every thing swam before me, and on asking for a drink of water a blackguard offered to —— in my mouth, nor could all my entreaties procure a drop of water. I would have given 1000 dollars for a basinful if I had had them. I only got laughed at for asking. I was not allowed to cover my legs, and was kept here about one hour and a half, the gunner and others from our prison were brought to look at me, and told I was a *pilan*. Before taking us back the locks were taken off our handcuffs, and they were secured by a piece of redhot iron. A blacksmith being brought for the purpose. With a deal of entreaty I got my leg-irons opened a little, but they were still very close, more so than any others. I asked for a chair to go back in. This was allowed me if I paid for it, which I willingly did. I was not allowed to speak to the carpenter, but he told Mr. Roope that all our fellow-prisoners were beheaded; Mr. Gully among the rest. This I was certain was a lie, and I have since heard that they have all been removed to some other place near the Tygin's, except Newman, who is with the carpenter, &c. No one I am glad to say was flogged but me, the three lascars not even put in irons. I am convinced this torture was inflicted in consequence of letters, as we this morning heard that the mandarins had heard from Amoy; that they were in a great fright, and that they daily expected the ships which were there to come over here. If they do come it is said we shall be given up. I wish to God they would try it.

September 9th.—Last night I got the soldiers who guard us to pull one of our hands out of irons. I have just written the above account of our late visit to Quan, I now go on. The weather has been mostly fine. We are truly on short allowance of every thing, having a basin of rice, and a fish about the size of a sprat, twice a day. The mandarin promised in ten days to let us out of irons again. To-day is the twelfth, but no signs of it. I believe the man to whom I am indebted not a little, keeps the money allowed us for food for himself. I have written to the lee lotier, but as usual he is out. We are badly off indeed.

18th.—These few days past, fine weather. Several Chinamen have applied to me for advice and medicine; some of whom I have cured, others getting better, and thus we get a little cash which helps to improve our food. Yesterday an old man, weak and reduced from a long-continued abuse of opium, came. I told him I had no medicine that would do him any good, nor was there any in Ty-wan, but if he liked I would give him a chit which if taken to Amoy, and given to some of the English ships there, they would send me some medicine. This he readily promised, and explained to me that for fear of its being found out he would put it in a package. I wrote accordingly to Forbes or any one it might be given to, and this morning he sent for it. God send it safe across, and grant us a speedy answer! We are still the same, being heavily ironed about the legs, and allowance of food short; nor is there any chance of a change taking place in our way of living, that I can see.

25th.—Continued fine weather. Nothing worth mentioning occurs except having my irons opened a little, in consequence of my feet and legs swelling; and this I was obliged to pay for; although the man was ordered to do it, he would not till paid for the job. He has robbed us, and continues to do so as much as possible. We employ ourselves drawing and painting, and occasionally I give advice and medicine; the fees for which assist our small allowance, and are very acceptable. Still no change nor any hint of one, neither have I heard from or of our fellow-shipmates. Legs and arms not yet well. I am told by several people that it was Quan's intention to break my arm, and that I am indebted to the lee lotier for his not doing so. This old "gent" has more than once showed us a little kindness, which I trust I may one day be able to repay—as well as Quan.

October 12th.—Continued fine weather. This morning the lee lotier came, bringing with him the carpenter and shroff, both clean shaved. He wanted to know the name of the English mandarin at Amoy.

I did not know. The carpenter persists in saying that the other three Chinese have been killed, and will not speak about the rest of our people. All I can get from him is that he will tell me all when we get to the ship. He is still in a great fright. They were taken away again directly. In the afternoon Heen, the one-eyed man, came and told us as much by signs as words, that out of both ships' companies Newman and ourselves were the only survivors. They were all taken out and beheaded about two or three days after our removal to the granary. This dreadful butchery has made us all most miserable. Poor Gully was the first who suffered. I believe a day before the rest. I cannot make out why Newman and we have been kept so long. Heen says that the mandarin did not kill us as we are the principal people belonging to the vessels, and that now peace has been proclaimed we shall be sent away. To us as yet all is a mystery. I shall not consider our lives worth a straw till we are out of their hands. Should we ever live to get clear and tell our sad tale, surely the British government will take notice of such wholesale murders—197 men were put to death in one day, most of them British subjects, and all serving under our flag. To add to our present wretched state of mind, the ship sailed this afternoon without having, as we are told, delivered her despatches in consequence of the Tinty not going to have an audience with her commander. This evening, we have a jacket and pair of trousers given to each of us, the best we have had yet. We receive also two plates of sweetmeats from the mandarin, with a promise of more food.

14th.—Fine weather. Day passed the same as yesterday. In the evening Mr. Roope, Partridge, and myself were taken out without being ironed to a gentleman on Quan's establishment, for the purpose of drawing. We saw the carpenter, shroff, and Newman, and heard that Heen's story was but too true, and Newman tells me the following account of it as all he knows:—Two or three days after we were taken away from our old hovel at Quan's, some of the mandarins' clerks went to their prison just at daylight, and gave them cash. Newman suspected all was not right, in consequence of having heard the day before that poor Gully had been killed. He says, he got up and saw the yard full of chairs, on each of which was a ticket in front. He sent for a pot of samshu and drank it all himself, telling his companions if they wanted any to buy it themselves, as he would give them none of his. After a short time they were put in irons, and each placed in a chair. He saw many soldiers with bloody clothes in their hands. These men went on ahead, and some others told him they were going to be beheaded. He was half-drunk from the grog he had taken, and on the way he broke off his hand and leg irons. At one place which they passed, the head mandarin was seated on a chair, and on reaching that place, he saw the Topas and Cassaib, who had got their irons off, kicking up a row. They told him the people were taking them all to be killed, and they would not be ironed. Newman persuaded them to let their irons be put on quietly, as, if they did not, they would be tortured and afterwards cut in a thousand pieces. They were then ironed and taken away. Newman, however, would not be ironed, and showed fight to two mandarins; and on turning round, for the first time, saw the head mandarin seated on a chair. He immediately began chin-chinning him and cow-towing, singing out all the time "Tywanfoo, Tywanfoo." He then stood upon his head. When the mandarin saw this, he said he was a good man,* and ordered him to be taken back. On the way back he broke the chair, and was taken into a house and heavily ironed, and then taken back to the prison. He thought we were all killed, and for four or five days did nothing but drink. He was alone at this time. When he heard that we were alive, he asked to come and live with us, but was refused. However, they sent him to a China prison, where he saw the carpenters, and with them he lived till now. He is now living at Chu Sam y ats's. The heads of our unfortunate fellow-

* Knocking the head on the ground is the sign in China of submission to authority. The mandarin manifestly thought that standing on the head was carrying this deferential submission to the extreme.

captives, the carpenter tells me, are placed at equal distances along the sea-shore on posts.

16th.—Taken up again to draw. In the afternoon each had a cap and pair of stockings given him. After which we went to the Bluebutton's to dinner. On arriving there we were taken to a small joss-house on his establishment. Shortly after he came. We all immediately cow-towed him. He told us that the late murders had been done by order of the emperor; that the mandarins here could not do so of their own accord; if they could they would not have kept them so long, but killed them directly. He said we were going to Amoy, and told us we must be quiet in the junk. He then asked me to draw him some pictures, which I promised. He said he would give me a kumshaw if I would make them handsome: he then went away; and we sat down to an excellent dinner and abundance of wine. After dinner we drank the queen, the emperor, and Bluebutton's health, and went home. Chairs had been provided for us. On going away we again chin-chinned the Bluebutton.

20th.—A fine day. Employed as before by the gentleman at Quan's place. In the afternoon we are taken to the Toti-Tygin to chin-chin him. He told us the same yarn as the Bluebutton about our unfortunate companions. He says he is glad we are going away, and thinks it will be in four or five days; and he told me if I liked to write a letter to the English ships at Amoy, he would send it for me, to tell them we are coming. This I promised to do. He says I must tell them not to send any ships here. Tells us a long yarn about the care he has taken of us, and told Newman that Joss had a good heart for him, and had saved his head. He said all the things that had been got from the wreck had been sent to the emperor, and that now he had paid the English a great deal of money. He also said he would tell the Poon Hoo to give us 200 dollars to buy provisions with, to take on board the junk with us. I having heard that he was ruptured, told him if I could get a truss at Amoy I would send it to him. He is head civil mandarin on the island, and has behaved more kindly to us than any of the others. He seems to be much better liked than the rest. After all this we are sent to get our dinner, which we do, and return home.

21st.—Fine weather. I write the promised letter. Make it as short as possible, as I have no doubt it will be read before the English get it. Am very careful what I say in it. I also write one which is to be sent to the emperor, thanking him for the care he has taken of us, and for sending us away, &c. I am to say in it how well the To Ty had behaved to us all: this is at their own request. To-day is a great day. Lots of chin-chinning going on; and in the afternoon a splendid procession well worth seeing.

25th.—Fine still. Mr. Roope and self drawing still. We receive two dollars each for two pictures, from Bluebutton. In the evening visit the China prison in which Newman and the carpenters were confined, where I ordered some baskets to be made for me. While there, Heen (the one-eyed man), who is jailer here, gave Mr. Roope a small piece of paper, which, on examination, proved to be two lines of poor Gully's log; the last, I suppose, he had ever written, being dated August 10th. He said he got it from one of the soldiers, who had either stolen it from him after death, or had it given to him. He also had an old shirt. I told Heen I would give him 100 dollars if he could find me any more such papers. He promised to make inquiry.

28th.—On going to Chu Sam y ats's, we are told we cannot go till to-morrow, as there is no place for us to sleep at Ampion; but that we are to be up early to-morrow, that we may go direct to the junk—delays are dangerous. No drawing to-day—performance still going on. Am told it will be very grand to-night. Some great chin-chin day with them. Quan has to-day a very large party—I counted twenty-six at dinner, which is laid in an exposed place, opposite the stage where they had performances. Chu Sam y ats tells us to stop till it is all over, that we may chin-chin Quan for the last time. Do so accordingly. The performance of to-day was, I think, entirely of a religious nature. At first, from not understanding it, thought it dull. The after-piece, if I may so call it, was a representation of the different ways of torturing and death which the Celestials practise. At about 2 a. m., all having gone, we chin-chin Quan for the last time. He tells us this is a bad place for ships to come to, &c.

29th.—About 5 a. m. are called to go to Chu Sam y ats's, from whose house we start. Go out at the nearest gate, and on coming to the beach, embark. Chin-chin old Chu Sam y ats, and start for the junk. The island of Ampion is about two miles from where we embarked. The place is very shallow, as we had in many places to get out and force the boat over the mud, the water not being more than one foot deep. About 10 a. m. get on board the junk.

November 3d.—Fine weather: wind more to the north-eastward. While weighing about 4 a. m. were roused out by the report of a gingal and an alarm of pirates, three of which had, I am told, been hovering about us, and would give no answer when hailed. However, we saw no more of them. At 9 saw the Pescadores, and about noon have them east by north. A fine moderate breeze.

The coast of Formosa from Tywanfoo up to abreast the Pescadores is very low, and there are many shoals off it. We were often in six feet water when the shore was not in sight, and work up by the lead, tacking by the sounding. Breakers were to be seen in several places, a long way off shore; at sunset came to, and in the evening, when the tide served, weighed and went round the next point of land to join our consort, who outsails us. About 9 came to again close to her. In the afternoon great preparations made for resisting piratical attacks; (we are told these islands are nests of piratical thieves;) firing guns occasionally to let the natives know we had arrived. The mandarins in a bit of a fright.

5th.—The tides among these islands, I should say, very irregular, and very strong at the springs. There are many good anchorages among the islands; as far as I can see and judge, all the people are very poor.

10th.—About this time two small war-junks came here from the mainland of China, bringing with them a report that four large English ships had left Amoy full of troops, and were going to Tywanfoo to attack the place. Our mandarins on hearing this were very anxious for the junk to go back, but this I would on no account consent to; I tried all means in my power to make the captain of the junk start off for Amoy; entreaty and threat were alike of no avail. We now began to be seriously alarmed and kept our eyes about us for any thing near in the shape of a boat to make our escape in. I am sure we should all have trusted our lives to any, even the smallest boat, rather than have hazarded a return to our late horrid place of imprisonment; and I declared to the mandarins, that if the junk attempted to go back I would stay on these islands, as would the rest of my fellow-prisoners.

At last, on the 24th of November, we got the captain of the junk to make a start. I firmly believe it was in consequence of our constantly ridiculing the qualities of his vessel that he then put to sea, and I have no doubt in my own mind that he would have put back had it not been for our laughing at him and his junk, and telling him what an English ship would do. The next morning, about seven or eight o'clock, we saw Chapel Island, near the port of Amoy. We fetched to leeward of the island and commenced working up to windward, or rather trying to do so, for we scarcely gained a bit of ground; at last he came to with an old broken anchor. This I told him at first would not hold the vessel, but he persisted in dropping it; the consequence was, that away we drove to leeward, had to weigh it again and drop another. We now learnt for the first time, that the mandarins did not intend to take us to Amoy, but wanted to land us either at Quemoy, to the northward of Amoy, or at a small town to leeward. Our informant was one of the junkmen; he told us that if the captain took the junk to either of these places, not to leave her or go on shore with the mandarins on any account, as they wished to pass us to the northward, and if they managed to do this, we should be all murdered at

Foo Chow Foo. This information, coupled with the little I could understand of the constant talking between the captain and mandarins, and the looks of the junkmen, caused us the most painful anxiety. We agreed to watch for any vessel during the night, and I wrote a small note which our friend the junkman was, if possible, to put into a fishing-boat during the night should one come near, which was a very likely thing to occur, the coast about there, and indeed all parts of it, swarming with fishing-boats of all sizes. I promised him fifty dollars on its delivery on board any British vessel in Amoy. I then got among the crew, and told them to insist on going to no other port, and that if it came to the worst they would stand by us; for this they were to receive among them a hundred dollars. It was my full intention, had the junk been put before the wind for the port under her lee, to have made a sudden attack on the mandarins and troops, and either killed or pitched them overboard; in this the seamen would have, I know, assisted us, as they detest and despise the mandarins and soldiers; they gave us some billets of wood for arms, these with men in our situation were not weapons to be despised; another thing in our favour was that most of the troops were sea sick, and might easily have here disposed of. I then went to the captain of the junk, and asked him whether he was going to Amoy. He said the mandarins had ordered him to go to another port, and he must do as they told him, or he should be squeezed (that is, have to pay a heavy fine). I assured him that if he went to any other harbour than Amoy, none of us would leave the junk, unless by force, and that I would cut her cable and let her drive on shore, when I could get a fishing-boat and sail to Amoy. After a little time all the crew came aft, and refused in a body to weigh the anchor if the junk was not to go to Amoy; that their agreement was for that port, and they would go to no other. The mandarins told them they only wanted to go a little way and land us, when the vessel would immediately proceed to her destined port. It was now my turn to speak, and I assured them, as I had the captain, that nothing but force should make us leave the junk in any other place than Amoy; that the mandarins on Formosa told us we were to go there, and there I insisted on being landed. After the noise occasioned by all speaking at once, a very common practice among the lower orders of Chinese, I went into the captain's little cabin, and promised him, if he took us straight to Amoy in the morning, I would give him 100 dollars, a dollar being the nearest road to a Chinaman's heart. He at last promised, on condition that I would make it appear to the mandarins that it was on account of the crew, and at the same time say nothing about the money, telling me that if they knew it they would take all from him, this of course

I readily promised, and left him, keeping as anxious a watch during the night that the junk did not drive to leeward as ever I did in my life. Morning at last dawned, when we saw a ship and a schooner running out of Amoy Harbour, and steering for Macao, the tide at length turned, and up came our anchor. Sail was made, and we worked to windward towards our long-looked for port of liberation, and at about 7 p.m., we passed some shipping at anchor, but too far off for us to make them hear, which we had resolved to do had they been any thing like within hail. It was quite dark, so there was no chance of our being seen. On getting further up the harbour a China boat came alongside, into which Mr. Roope, the gunner, and others jumped, the soldiers trying to stop them. I stood by the rope, and when they were in let go, telling them to make for the nearest ship, which they did. I was now satisfied in my own mind that we should soon have boats for the rest of us, the junk anchored about eight, when I told the mandarins I wanted to go on board one of the ships, this they refused, telling me I must go on shore with them in the morning. I said I would not remain, but gave them my word that I would return the next morning. Finding they could not keep me, for I told them I would jump overboard, they allowed me to go. I soon got on board an English vessel, and found out where some of my friends were; to their ships I immediately went, and was most kindly welcomed by my friends and countrymen, who had given up all hopes of ever seeing us again.

The same evening I saw Sir H. Pottinger, and gave him an account of what had occurred, as well as my notes taken while in prison, a verbatim copy of which he has since had. He received us very kindly, and offered us some clothing, which thanks to my personal friends I had no need of. The ward-room officers of H. M. Brig "Pelican" generously sent some clothes for all of us, with a kind note, begging our acceptance of them. The present itself was exceedingly acceptable, but it was rendered doubly so by the very handsome manner in which the offer of it was conveyed. I felt this kind behaviour most deeply at the time, and not the less so because of the striking contrast it offered to the treatment of which I had for so many months been a victim. I cannot refer to the circumstance without taking advantage of the opportunity thus afforded me publicly to express my sincere obligations to those who at that moment so cordially manifested their sympathy for us.

Sir H. Pottinger offered us a passage down in the steamer "Pluto," the captain and officers of which vessel vied with each other in acts of kindness never to be forgotten by me.

Thus were we liberated on the 26th of November, having been prisoners since the 10th of March, and had the war not have ended as it did, our heads were destined to ornament the walls or gates of the imperial city of Pekin.

I kept my word with the mandarin, and went on board in the morning, but found that they and all the soldiers had fled during the night, for fear of being killed by the English; so the junkmen told us. I paid the money to all as I had promised; 50 dollars to the man with the letter; 100 dollars to the crew; and 100 dollars to the captain.

LETTERS

WRITTEN BY

MR. GULLY TO CAPTAIN DENHAM.

I.

June 12, 1842.

My dear Denham,

I wrote you yesterday by Heen, the one-eyed man, telling you of my having written to the lotier on the 10th, "and of our having 46 cash served out to each yesterday." After he left, the lotier's head man came and turned two executioners out of the room opposite to our old place, and gave them to Mr. Partridge, the gunner, and myself; and now I think we are as well off as yourself, but I would of course sooner be with you. I think you would like this place better than your own. The lotier sent us an extra quantity last night of roast pork, same as before, and in the morning one mace was served out to each man. This looks well, if it lasts; of course I lay it all to my letter to the lotier, but I can't make out how he read it unless you stood interpreter Remember me to Roope and all your fellow prisoners, and tell Zu Quang Leon to come and see us soon. My finger still bad. I sent your handkerchief by Heen. Why did you not write by him? He had an excellent opportunity of delivering my letter, and can do so now without risk. All well, and the samshu has cured the piles. Our folks have not exceeded yet. If you want an excuse for sending, send my steamer, if Roope will let it come. God bless you, and hurrah! for a speedy deliverance. If you were here, or I with you, I'd keep your spirits up. Any news of the *railway* and *the waterfall?* We hear you are allowed one mace a day each, Mr. Partridge and the gunner desire their good wishes to be conveyed, and believe me,

Yours sincerely,

ROB. GULLY.

We hear that John Williams is dead. I open this again because I have not, I think, expressed my wish to be with you in sufficiently strong terms. Do your best, I can do little at present, as they have granted all I have asked, but I may have an opportunity soon.

To Captain Denham.

II.

June 19, 1842.

Dear Denham,

I got your letter of the 11th only yesterday.

I was getting anxious from not hearing from you. Heen promises to be here to-morrow for this chit. If you think there is any risk on your side in sending and receiving these chits, drop it at once until you receive a letter from the other side of the water. The yarn about our living together is all nonsense, depend upon it. The musquito curtains are rather too much. In the letter I sent you yesterday I told you about our new habitation. We are all right, and all but clear of lice. Two or three more days will do it. I am happy to say the people have been behaving better since we were separated. José Dias has been very sick for the last three days. I am amusing myself painting sea views, &c. I have begun the taking of Chusan, and nearly finished a tiger hunt. I have got an awful sheet of paper to commence Chin Hae upon. All this passes away the time. The tiger hunt I have promised to Heen, so you will most likely see it. Do try your best to get me with you, for I am heartily tired of Mr. Partridge, he is a perfect nuisance; besides, I flatter myself that you are in better spirits when I am with you. I had a horrid attack of piles yesterday, and the gunner has been laid up for two or three days in the same way. However, we are comparatively comfortable. Why does not Zu Quang Leon come to see me in my new abode. Our old jailer has turned quite civil. You may imagine that I have very little to write about

We drank the Duke of Wellington's health last night, it being the anniversary of the battle of Waterloo. Remember me kindly to Roope, and all in your *hole*, and tell the former not to tear his shirt. Send me a small piece of gamboge to show our boy what yellow paint is. We have no cash left to buy samshu, so I am expecting a precious attack of piles. God bless you. If any thing occurs before Heen comes I will add to this.

Yours sincerely,

R. GULLY.

To Captain Denham.

III.

June 21, 1842.

Dear Denham,

Your letter of the 18th arrived all safe yesterday, and I sent you another in return; but you must understand I can't answer your letters the day I receive them, or I should probably be discovered. I am sorry the departure of the junk-man was delayed, for I doubt very much whether he would trust another with the letter. If an opportunity occurs of course I shall write across, but I have no hopes of any thing of the sort. We hardly ever see a soul except the people of the establishment. I don't believe a word of the report about taking us away from the town, but should they try it I will refuse to go until I see you. I think we could make a fight of it here, and perhaps get the assistance of the Bengalese. Can't you get the shroff a licking the next time you are up; don't spare him. I wish I could get to live with you. I have been sick for three days. Mr. Partridge is such a cursed fidget, and annoys me by skylarking with every Chinese blackguard he can get hold of. Our fellow-prisoners, the sea-cunnies, had a row with the jailer last night after we were locked up, but I don't know the cause. The row brought down the mandarin's head man and others. By the by, Ayum talked nonsense about our mandarin being greater than yours. Your fellow's the Quan Chow foo, or mayor of the city, and on grand occasions wears a white button. If we do get to live together, I don't think we shall have any trouble in getting the letters from Amoy when they come. It is just daylight, and I am writing to be ready for Heen, who promises to be here to-day with some gamboge. He has got his tiger hunt, which I hope Mr. Roope will say is a very *spirited production.* If he does not, tell him he's no judge. I agree with you about hearing some good this month, for I don't see any thing to prevent the Macao people from sending our traps, beer, and other necessaries. I heard a shotted gun fired the other night; I suppose the fellows are practising. I have nothing more to say except to beg you to continue your exertions to get me with you as soon as possible, and I trust you will be successful. It all rests with your mandarin.

Yours sincerely,
R. GULLY.

I forgot to say we have not heard the report about leaving this town, except from you. It is all nonsense, they would be too happy to get rid of us, unless the parties demanding us also demand the dollars, &c., which were in the "Ann." Fine breeze this for the ships coming up. We must hear something soon. God preserve you all.

To Captain Denham.

IV.

June 27, 1842.

My Dear Denham,

I received yours of the 22d only yesterday evening, by Heen, and was very sorry to learn from him that you are very sick; from what I can make out from him you have a kind of bloody flux. It is a disease very common over India, where the water is bad. If you have it, you must insist upon having good water, or you will never get rid of it. It is common in all the Dutch settlements. I hope you are, however, better by this time. It might be a good opportunity to get me with you, if you were to say that I understood a little doctor's pigeon. They would, perhaps, believe it, for I don't stand doctors here. I trust your illness will not put your visit off for any length of time. I can't get to see our lotier at any price. The scoundrel is actually starving us; and his attendants say, that your fellow is a fool for treating you so well. I have had continued rows for the last ten days, but of no use. I believe he is bent upon flogging me. If you hear any thing of the sort, you must kick up a row, on my account; for you may depend upon it, if they succeed (which I doubt), I shall not be the last one. I had a row with the old jailer yesterday, for using dirty language while drunk with opium. Your description of the securities of your place of abode is highly amusing. What are the Macao people about? I did expect to hear from them before this. Your plan about the letters is good; but I doubt if they will be able to read mine. I am very glad Quat is with you. Heen seems to be trustworthy, but he did not bring the gamboge. Glad you like the tiger hunt. The action of the purple horse was inimitable. I trust your new place of abode is ornamented with the Beelzebub steam-frigate. I finished Chusan (the taking of it), and my necessities compelled me to part with it. I kept it for Zu Quang Leon for the space of a week. It was really like the place, and the fellows running away quite natural. I should have liked him to have it, only he does not seem inclined to come near us. I have nearly finished Chin Hae, and intend to begin Amoy and the Bogue, when I have finished a large picture of elephants, &c., that is ordered. It is nearly done. Remember me to Roope and all your fellow-prisoners. I can't believe the 10th of next month will pass without hearing from Amoy; if it does I shall go mad. I am getting as thin as a lath, really from having nothing to put into my mouth. I trust I may some day or other have a chance of paying this villain off. We are entirely clear of small vermin, and have been so for a week. This is indeed a blessing. I shall most likely add to this before I send it. Hoping it will find you quite recovered,

Believe me, yours sincerely,

R. GULLY.

29th.—My spirits have been raised only to be depressed again. Your lotier paid ours a late visit on Monday evening, and all his attendants told me, without being asked, that I was going in the morning to see you. It was false, our rascal gets worse and worse. Nothing but rows, bad living, treatment, and every thing else. Some ship ought to be here. This is beautiful weather for them. I am improving fast in drawing, and have just finished a face which would astonish you as much as it has me. I think I should, on getting clear of this, set up artist at Macao; but Chinnery is an old man, and I don't wish to take the bread out of his mouth. Chin chin to Roope.

2d July.—Nothing new, getting very anxious to hear concerning your health. The Chinese have only just found out that I am an artist. Lots of orders, consequently lots of small coin. The gunner considers it beneath a native of the first "*Nation in the World*" to work for necessaries.

V.

July 4, 1842.

Dear Denham,

I am sorry to have to inform you that José Maria, in one of his cowardly fits of passion, struck a poor boy in the side, who used to run errands for us. This was on the 2d instant. He spit blood at the time, and we have been told that he died during the night. For God's sake write and tell me how to act. The mandarins have done nothing as yet. The boy had been complaining of a pain in his side for some time before. I have no doubt he would not have lived very long, but of course the blow accelerated his death. It was a cruel and cowardly action, and the worst thing that could have happened. If they only take one head for it, I shall consider myself lucky.

R. GULLY.

VI.

July 6, 1842.

Dear Denham,

Heen brought the letter begun by Mr. Roope and finished by yourself, on the 4th instant, after you had been to the lotier's (Bluebutton's). I sent a few words in return, to say that I had sent you a set of chessmen cut out by Phillipe. I was very glad to hear of your recovery; you must take care of yourself, for it is a very dangerous disease; and mark my word, if you touch that bad water you will get it again. I was very sorry to hear of the conduct of the sea-cunnies. It would be bad enough anywhere, here it is worse; but not so bad as the conduct of that wretch José Maria. The poor boy came back yesterday, looking very ill, and what do you think? the brute not only did not show any signs of sorrow, but did not even ask how he was; on the contrary, tried to drive him away with all sorts of abuse; he and his friends. This put me out, and I flared up in glorious style. If you had only heard the Spanish, Portuguese, and Chinese, I rapped out, it would rather have astonished you. However I could not shame the villains. It ended in the boy coming in, but they had better not let me see them ill-treat him. After the row, the boy showed more good feeling than I had expected to see in a Chinaman. By the by, his object in coming, was to make friends with the whole of them; and he brought some mangoes to give them, which makes their conduct ten times worse: but they are a bad set except José Dias. I must tell you all my trouble. You know that our lotier promised Mr. Roope and the gunner, that we should have better food. Well, yesterday morning they brought us the same as usual, and I thought it a good plan to stick out until they gave us better as promised. All agreed, and we refused to eat any thing for *five minutes*, when the Yankee's stomach could stand it no longer, and he commenced operations. I had it all served out then, and told each man to act for himself. I threw mine out into the yard, and am going to write to the lotier this day, requesting either more food or a mace a day. I would rather have the former, for there are only two of us that would take the latter (Mr. Partridge and I), and a precious cook Mr. Partridge would make. I am doing pretty well in the artist line, and improving fast. All the yarn about Jam Sin must be nonsense. Don't tell Roope, but in his letter he says that Domingo has had no "piece" since you left. Remember me kindly to Roope. What are the Macao people about? I have felt better and stronger since the mangoes came in, than I have during the whole imprisonment. If I understand you right, you are in the house we were smoking at one day, not in the bamboo house. I have done my best to get to you, but I really believe that the fools think me some great personage, and shirk me accordingly, because they are afraid of finding it out.* The shroff, perhaps, has told them some wonderful yarn. However, I shall not give it up, but mention it in my letter to the lotier. God bless you, and tell

* It would seem from his being murdered with the common sailors, and from the fact of every one called an officer, even the gunner, being spared, that the reverse was the case. He held no office—so the Chinese thought nothing of him.

Roope to write as well as yourself. I shall add to this if any thing takes place. Yours,

R. GULLY.

VII.

July 8, 1842.

Dear Denham,

I add this small postscript to tell you that we have just heard that another vessel has been wrecked. We heard it from tolerable Chinese authority; but the party could give us no particulars, except that it happened three days ago. We have had a continuation of flares up since you were at the Bluebutton's, because the lotier would not perform his promise about giving more food. Four basins, one tub, and a plate. Last night, Mr. Partridge slipped out unknown to me, and went up to where the lotier was lounging in his chair, (much to his astonishment,) told him of his promise, requested that he would perform it, or send us to live with you. He promised when the rain is over to give us better. He was in a good humour, and I really think the fellow is very poor. I prevented Mr. Partridge from going in the morning, and had I known of his intention in the evening, of course, I should have either accompanied him or stopped him.

Since writing the above, I have heard the story of the shipwreck from several quarters, and I place so much credit in it, that I think you had better mention it in your next letter across the water.

They say that all hands are drowned, and that it was at Tamsing or Khelan. I can't make out where, but if there is such a place as Tamsin Khelan, it is there. Perhaps you will be able to find out. The big guns commenced a new system of feeding last night, and at last we have more than enough to eat, very good. I am afraid the mangoes have done me no good. Did you see the eclipse last night. No strangers allowed to see us. Yours,

R. GULLY.

VIII.

July 11, 1842.

Dear Denham,

I sent you a letter, yesterday evening, by Heen, who came here bringing two letters from the sea-cunnies, and none from you, which was pleasant. He said you told him you were coming to see me to-day. I hope it is true, but don't believe it. Here have I been doing all sorts of things to induce my lotier to send me to you, and at last have got him to promise to ask Quan (your fellow) who being the higher mandarin of the two, must be consulted. The sea-cunnies, at your place, have heard some absurd story about five Tamsin being licked until they declared that they took us by fighting; they need not do that. They have only to say that we were taken by fighting to satisfy the authorities on the main. I expect it to be another yarn of that villain of a shroff, who, I trust, will lose his head yet.

Here is the 10th of July over, and no news from Macao.

Yours,

R. GULLY.

IX.

July 12, 1842.

My Dear Denham,

Yours of the 10th I received yesterday, by Mr. Partridge. "It is a long lane that has no turning; when things are at the worst they mend." I think we have proved those two proverbs to be true. From the account I get from Mr. Partridge and the gunner, the Redbutton must be a trump, or else he must have received a hint from Amoy. The letter tallies with the story I mentioned in my last, of a ship having been here and gone again. Quan's love for the English in general, and you in particular, also looks like it, as well as the seizure of the papers; and the question asked you by the Redbutton yesterday. I was to have had a sight of him to-day, but the rain is a stopper. Our mandarin has been to chin chin him this morning, and we are to go to-morrow. We must do our best to persuade him to make us members of his establishment with a liberal salary. This is not what I want to write about though, in case Heen comes before we meet. I wish you seriously to turn it over in your mind, whether it will not be better, if he asks me if I have written to Amoy, to say yes, that I wrote from the town halfway between this and Tamsin, and that I have received no answer, because I told them not to write to me, but to write to the mandarin. This will put them on a wrong scent, and perhaps get our friend the Brassbutton into a row. Think of it; our junk friend, when he brings the answer, must take care what he is about, for they will be on the look out unless put on another scent. I have heard no particulars about the shipwreck, but the man who told us of it, says he thinks it to be true; he is the best man I have seen about here; quite a Zu Quang Leon in a little way. I am sorry to hear of your health, and that of Roope being bad. I tell you it is the water, but you won't believe me. If you don't drink it you cook with it. I think it not improbable, if they intend looking after us, that they have detained the junk-man to act as pilot; which will account for your not receiving my answer from Captain Forbes. Tell the carpenter to tell the yarn about not ransoming us to the marines. The mandarins ought to be exceedingly obliged to us for promoting them. Yours,

R. GULLY.

X.

July 14, 1842.

Dear Denham,

I finished my picture of the capture of Amoy yesterday, the whole army was drowned this morning by an inundation. The rain not only comes through the roof, but we have numerous miniature waterfalls through the walls. We have got some paper for Roope, and tell him to bring some cash with him to pay for it, when he is taken up before the mandarins again. There that will do for the present. Yours sincerely,

R. GULLY.

16th.—Aticoa, our Chinese friend, still persists in his yarn about the shipwreck; he says, that no men have been brought here yet, but that we shall know more about it by and by. What a heavenly day yesterday was. Nothing new. Since writing the above, I have been told by two Chinamen that there is a foreign ship here. Neither of the parties, however, in my opinion is such good authority as Aticoa, who says he knows nothing about it. You must endeavour to find out if it is true or not. I have little doubt of the shipwreck, and from the delay in bringing the crew here, or correct information, I am in hopes it is a man-of-war, and that the crew have landed with their arms and *munitions* of war, and are showing the valiant Tywan troops some pretty sport. I am better on the whole. All hands are allowed to cut their whiskers and beards to their liking. I think I shall [never] get better as long as I am here. I have been on my back all day. This is some great day among the mandarins; our fellows have had a feast of stewed beef, cakes, and tobacco.

We hear we are to get our new clothes to-morrow. I will send a paper of tobacco for Mr. Roope before breakfast.

Yours sincerely,

R. GULLY.

XI.

July 24, 1842.

Dear Denham,

This morning your mandarin and another paid us a visit, and the shroff and mestry came with them. They had all the Nerbudda's people up, and asked them their ages, &c., and then Mr. Partridge was sent for, who said we were all getting sick for want of proper exercise. That we had not received the clothes promised, and that we wanted to be allowed to walk about the yard, or we should some of us die; to which they answered, they had received an order for three of us to go and live with Red-button, and that we were going in five or six days; that our clothes were not yet finished, but that we should have them when we went to Redbutton's. I was sorry to hear from the mestry of the death of two of the crew, but it is a good sign their having permitted the remainder of the crew their liberty, and looks as if the deaths had put them in a fright. I trust we shall be able to retaliate some day or other. I asked the mestry what the shroff had been telling the mandarins. He said he could not tell me then, but would if we ever got free. I have been in a very desponding state for the last two or three days; sick and disappointed at our not going to Redbutton's to live together. It is an odd idea that these people should now think of asking the ages names, &c. of the Nerbudda's people, after having had them on the island nine or ten months. Never mind, old fellow, our troops are in Pekin now, or else a proper treaty is in course of signature; I hope the former. Remember me to Roope. Nothing of Heen. I don't place much confidence in going to Redbutton's, because the clerks here say, we are to have the clothes when the cold comes.

XII.

July 27th, 1842.

Dear Denham,

I received yours of yesterday's date by the pipe-bearer, and just had time to give him one of rather an old date in return. Now begin another in case Heen should come with either of your former letters. The pipe-bearer seems a decent fellow. I have promised him a picture if he takes my letter to you; if he takes my letter to you pray do him one of some sort; I will if I can—but I have so much difficulty in getting paints and decent paper. Roope will help you *if not too unwell*, or his appetite should not fail him. I am sorry to hear that you are bad again, but I hope it is not so serious as the last. Believe me, I cannot express in language my desire to be with you at Redbutton's. Hope deferred, maketh the heart sick indeed. We have been told the same yarn as yourself about furnishing the house. If I think it true, I doubt if "the wish is not father to the thought." They do tell such lies. If any ships are coming here this weather ought to tempt them. I suffer at night from nightmare more than I ever suffered awake. I don't think we shall be called up to translate your official letter, but if we are, depend upon our using all sorts of strong language to get to the furnished abode. Remember me to Roope, and say I have finished with his log, and am anxious to return it in case of accident. Shall I trust it with Heen or the other man? I shall not write again by the latter until I know that he has delivered the last safe. Where can Quan be gone to? I am happy to say that our opposite neighbours have been behaving very well lately, and now amuse themselves in the daytime very laudably by learning writing and arithmetic, in which I give them all the assistance I can. The people about here are civil, and the cook generally comes to know what we will have for dinner. All this is an improvement; but I want somebody to talk to. From disgust and want of paints and paper, I have not drawn any thing for a fortnight. The gunner is as well as usual, eats well, drinks *well* water, sleeps well, and smokes like a chimney. Mr. Partridge is like a young crow, but I am afraid he would not make so good a pie. No signs of the junkman. I am afraid the last chit did not go. God send that we may soon meet.

Believe me, yours, &c.

R. GULLY.

Won't I pay our jailers out. I am devising all sorts of places to save the log-books. I think the best way would be to say they were English joss pigeons.

28th.—After I had written the above, Heen came, and they let him in, but I immediately saw that he was suspected and watched, and acted accordingly by keeping aloof, unluckily he did not observe it. He was so narrowly watched by all three jailers that I could not give him a hint. In an attempt to give the letters to Isidore, he failed, and the letters were seen by two of the jailers, but they said nothing. The boy had been sent to the head jailer on Heen's first arrival. This fellow soon came and sat down opposite Heen, and there remained until he went away. When the head jailer came, Heen saw that he was watched, and acted very well. We kept the head jailer in talk until Heen went away, and glad I was to see him outside the gates, for I expected every minute to see him seized and searched. They have had a hint from somebody, and as Heen has not been here since you went to Redbutton's, I can't help coupling it with the question asked you. They, I have no doubt, think Heen is the channel through which we hear from Amoy. When he had gone, both the jailers swore they saw the letter, and told every body. I am afraid Heen is not yet safe, so give him a hint if you can; and if you send another letter, stuff it in a cake which the man can give Mr. Partridge without any chance of suspicion.

XIII.

July 29th, 1842.

Dear Denham,

The enclosed was prepared all ready for the pipe-bearer, but he was obliged to be so quiet in his movements that I could not give it him. Yours, of date 27th, came all safe. You have the same attack that I had. Try my cure, a mango, rind and all; it cured me, but the piles still vex me at times. From the distinctness with which we have heard the surf for the last thirty-six hours, I am sure that we are nearer the sea than we suspect, or that the surf is nearly as bad as at Madras. If you had told me who your informant was, I should be better able to judge concerning the truth of what you were told about our release. Go it, old fellow, and get us together, and then we will have a good growl. I am as peevish and fidgetty as yourself. It was Roope's log that made me of opinion that your last chit did not go, coupled with your getting no answer. Kind regards to Roope, and say I will not mention him in my next letter at all. I can't say I am sorry for what I said before, because he deserved it.

Yours, very sincerely,

ROBERT GULLY.

GLOSSARY OF TERMS USED IN THE DIARIES.

Cash—1200th part of a dollar.
Chin chew—Right.
Chow chow—Food.
Chunam—Lime.
Cunjee—Water that rice is boiled in.
Dungree—Very coarse cotton cloth.
Holau—Good man.
"How how."—"Good good."
Joss—Idol.
Joss Pigeon—Religious rites.
Joss houss—Church or temple.
Kentledge—Iron ballast.
Lotier—Mandarin.
Mace—100 cash.
Mestry—Good man.
Monghoon—A pungent kind of herb rolled up in paper, and burnt to drive mosquitoes away.
Norie—Norie's Epitome of Navigation.
Pelang—Beetle nut and leaf.
Pilau—Bad man.
Pown Hoo—One of the blue-button mandarin's titles.
Samshu—A kind of sour wine or spirit.
Sea-cunnies—European sailors.
Shroff—A money dealer—agent.
Sticks—A phrase used as if in counting, thus "about four sticks."
Tindal—Boatswain's mate.

C. WHITING, BEAUFORT HOUSE, STRAND.

For EU product safety concerns, contact us at Calle de José Abascal, 56–1°,
28003 Madrid, Spain or eugpsr@cambridge.org.

www.ingramcontent.com/pod-product-compliance
Ingram Content Group UK Ltd.
Pitfield, Milton Keynes, MK11 3LW, UK
UKHW012346130625
459647UK00009B/580

* 9 7 8 1 1 0 8 0 4 5 7 1 1 *